Sky

Backpacking

MAREK BIDWELL

UK Book Publishing.com

Skye Line

Editing, design, typesetting and publishing by UK Book Publishing

www.ukbookpublishing.com

ISBN: 978-1-917329-06-4

Mark Scholl

Scan this QR code to view colour versions of the photographs in this book, or search for Marek Bidwell's website on Substack where you will also find additional content and a link to the GPX route track.

CONTENTS

This book is dedicated to my only cousin

Stephen John Pollard

6th December 1968 – 4th March 2023

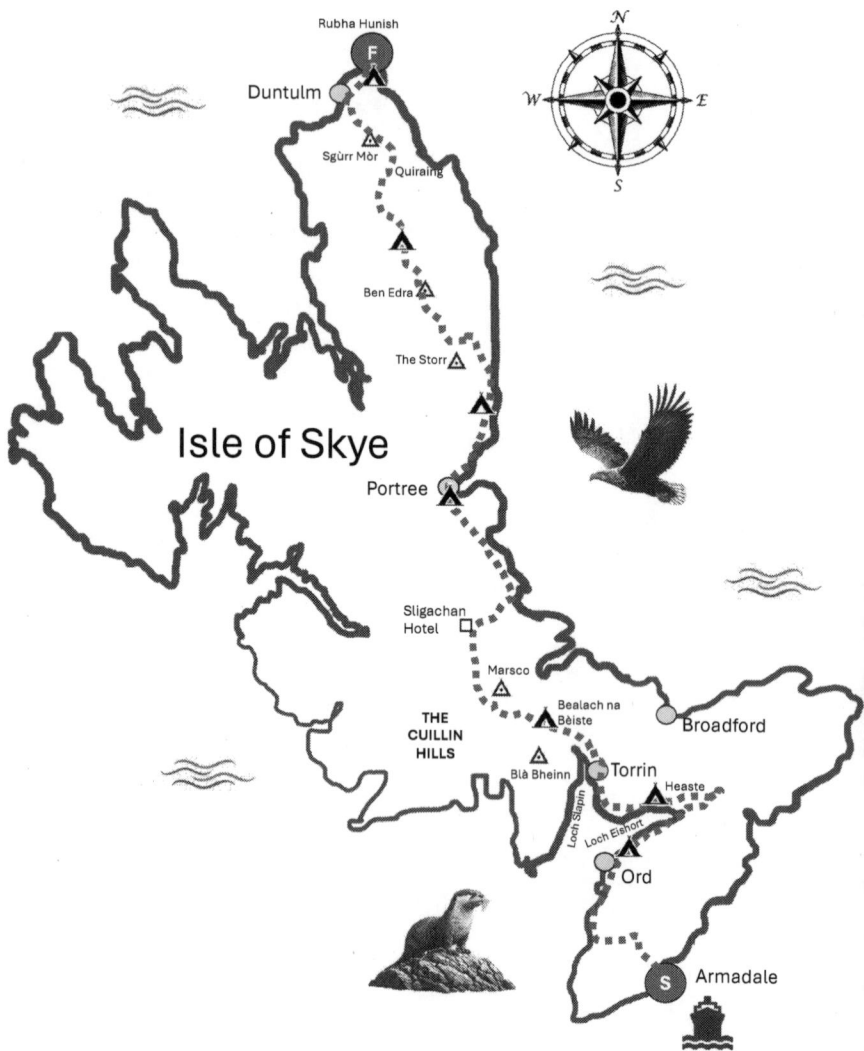

Rubha Hunish

F

Duntulm

Sgùrr Mòr

Quiraing

Ben Edra

The Storr

Isle of Skye

Portree

Sligachan
Hotel

Marsco

THE
CUILLIN
HILLS

Bealach na
Bèiste

Blà Bheinn

Broadford

Torrin

Heaste

Loch Slapin

Loch Eishort

Ord

Armadale

S

N

W   E

S

PREFACE

This book is written for two groups of people. Firstly, if you have never backpacked a long-distance trail, this is for you. From the comfort of your favourite chair or sitooterie, you will vicariously traverse a landscape of lochs and mountains and experience how the ever-changing vistas seep into your soul: rain and rainbows, dawn and dusk, windswept mountains, otters and eagles, sun and sea, and even the Northern Lights. It might even inspire you to give it a try.

Secondly, this book is for seasoned hikers who may wish to traverse the Isle of Skye on this route from south to north, proposed by photographer David Paterson in 1999: Armadale Ferry to Rubha Hunish. My descriptions will give you an insight into what this journey entails and how it differs from the conventional 'Skye Trail'. For you, there is also a detailed review of my lightweight kit at the end, along with tips on the route and a link to a gxp file of the path I took.

There is something here for everybody. So, *Trobhad!* (come with me)

1. A LONG WALK…

Not long after we were married, my wife and I hired a cottage at Kyleakin on the Isle of Skye, where the 'new', as it was then, road bridge landed. It was a great adventure – a world away from Newcastle upon Tyne, where we lived – to a land of myth and mountains. Tracy and I set off up the A1 after work on Friday evening and stopped for dinner when we crossed the border into Scotland, thinking we had made good progress. Long after dark, we were still winding our way across a pitch-black Rannoch Moor, the vast darkness swallowing the car's headlights. In the wee small hours, we crossed the bridge and found our accommodation.

Two things stand out in my mind from that trip. Firstly, two friends from Newcastle, both GPs, joined us for the first weekend – yes, we were also amazed when we discovered how far it was – and I climbed one of the Cuillins, Sgurr nan Gillean, with Mark, a seasoned mountaineer. Mark led the way, telling me we were on the tourist route, except for a diversion to do some bouldering over volcanic sandpaper rocks. Tracy recalled that I was terrified on the precipitous summit, which doesn't surprise me because, although I love hiking, I am afraid of heights. I had a similar acrophobic experience on top of the Duomo in Florence: the domed terracotta roof dropping away in all directions, an imagined experience of falling, grabbing smooth marble columns for reassurance. But on Skye, Mark had confidence for the both of us, and we made it to the top, and back.

My second memory of Skye is more tangible; in fact, it's sitting on my desk as I write: a technicolour photobook by David Paterson called *A Long Walk on the Isle of Skye* (that I'll refer to as *A Long Walk*). I must have picked it up in the bookshop in Portree, and as well as the panoramic landscapes, snowy mountains, and purple sunsets, I was smitten with the concept Paterson devised of walking continuously from the ferry landing at Armadale to the northern-most tip of the island at Rubha Hunish, where, in the author's words, 'The Western Isles line distant horizons, the rock, sky and ocean views are unparalleled, and the feeling of being at an end of the earth is irresistible'. Little did I know then that nearly a quarter-of-a-century later, I would wake up at two o'clock in the morning to answer the call of nature, extricate my much older body from a lightweight tent perched on top of the cliff at Rubha Hunish, to be greeted by the pale green Northern Lights ghosting over those isles at the end of the earth.

The reasons why it took me so long to fulfil that ambition boil down to a lack of time and resources whilst building my career as an Environmental Consultant, which in itself involved plenty of travelling, and the emotional wrench of tearing myself away from Tracy, who has other pastimes that don't include crawling into a tiny, cold tent. And – although I was in the Scouts at school, and some of my earliest memories are climbing mountains in the Lake District with my parents, jumping into boggy 'mellymows' with my sister, and being led on by the lure of Kendal Mint Cake – a solo expedition across a remote island just seemed out of my reach. Something that other people did: people in books, like Cheryl Strayed or Raynor Winn.

The trigger that catapulted me back into backpacking occurred four years ago when I was caring for Dorothy, an elderly friend and neighbour who, along with her since deceased sister, became our surrogate aunties when we first moved from Nottingham to Newcastle. Dorothy was gregarious: she loved nature, flower arranging, singing and travel, especially Kenya where she taught for many years. We had much in common. It was early July, and I needed a few days off but had no time to plan and didn't want to go far in case she deteriorated, so I caught the bus from Newcastle to Blyth and walked up the coast of Northumberland to Bamburgh. I borrowed a friend's army surplus bivvy bag, scavenged my old-school stove from the loft, and found a blue plastic sheet in the shed to erect above my head as a tarp. I was only away for four nights, but it was a transformative experience that led me to complete a circuit of Northumberland over the next two summers. Planning for and undertaking these hikes gave me a degree of resilience that, along with the support of family and friends, helped me cope with a string of difficult situations that lay ahead. On my return, Dorothy's condition deteriorated, and she passed away later that year, after which Tracy and I had to organise her affairs. While we were still grieving and trying to sell her house, the Covid lockdowns began, and everything ground to a halt. Emotional support was curtailed. Then, Tracy became ill and was left in limbo on a waiting list for three years, resulting in her finally having a major operation last year.

Backpacking around Northumberland didn't solve any of life's problems, but it gave me something to hold on to. Something that felt bigger than myself and rooted me in the landscape where I had lived since 1993: the same place where Dorothy was from, now my adopted home.

Put another way, a long hike is 'a whole-body enema', as sociologist Glen Bateman declares in Stephen King's *The Stand* as they trudge across plague-decimated North America.

2. HATCHING PLANS

Once my circuit of Northumbria was complete, I cast around for a new challenge, and David Paterson's book called to me from my bookshelf. Although I now had some backpacking experience, *A Long Walk on The Isle of Skye* still felt like a challenge because whereas Northumberland is familiar territory, Skye exudes an aura of rugged remoteness. If anything went wrong, I wouldn't be able to call on family to help, like the fateful night during the third leg of my Northumberland hike when I got food poisoning and Tracy drove all the way from Newcastle to the North Pennines to my rescue.

In the spring of 2022, I started planning in earnest by purchasing the 1:50,000 OS maps of north and south Skye and tracing the route that Paterson described in his book with a highlighter pen. His route descriptions give a general sense of direction but sometimes lack detail, so I had to guess some sections. Also, I later discovered that Paterson tended to understate the difficulties of the terrain. For example, when ascending to the highest point of the walk, a col ominously named 'Bealach na Bèiste' in the mountains between Torrin and Sligachan, he writes, 'Climb diagonally to the right, up steep but straightforward rocky slopes to the bealach which is wide and flat'; whereas, I found myself clinging to the rock whilst the weight of my backpack tried to somersault me backwards down the mountain. It didn't help that the good weather I'd enjoyed up to that point suddenly broke, and by the time I pitched my tent at around 1200 feet, there were near gale-force winds.

So, in an attempt to obtain more specific directions, I purchased the Cicerone guidebook *Walking the Skye Trail*, but this turned out to be a very different route across Skye, starting at Rubha Hunish in the north and ending ignominiously in the town of Broadford on the A87 in the south-west. While the two routes overlap in certain places, such as the Trotternish Ridge, I discarded the Skye Trail because it seemed to meander aimlessly, lacking the coherence of Paterson's singular aim of traversing the island from south to north, which facilitates arrival on the iconic Skye ferry. Nevertheless, I questioned my decision several times during the first few days whilst wading through vegetation, clambering over deer fences, and scrambling across gullies on the remote peninsula of Sleat. When I finally did join a path on the north shore of Loch Eishort at the ruined village of Boreraig, I couldn't contain my relief and nearly hugged a bemused hiker who informed me there was a Land Rover track all the way to Torrin.

As the summer of 2022 approached, I was more-or-less ready to go to Skye when my much-loved centenarian great-aunt Margaret passed away. So, instead of heading north, I trundled south to her funeral in Hertfordshire and remembered her long and fruitful life with family.

With plans postponed for another twelve months, I did several practice hikes in Cumbria with a new Vango tent, but I ground to a halt on the ridge up Kidsty Pike where I fell asleep, exhausted, on the narrow path and was woken up by a lady concerned I was unconscious. After that experience, I determined that my base weight of over 10kg was too heavy for my ageing, and often painful, back to haul 84 miles with more than 13,000 ft of ascent on Skye.

So, I lost myself in an enjoyable but expensive rabbit hole of upgrading and lightweighting my kit. After much research, I invested in a super lightweight trekking-pole tent made of a novel fabric called Dyneema, first developed as sail cloth for yachts and billed as 'the world's strongest fiber'. I imported the tent from a company in California, and despite being expensive and somewhat see-through, it turned out to be an excellent find, keeping me dry and midge-free and miraculously weighing only 607g. I made a minor modification to the tent in anticipation of the Scottish weather by adding four additional guy-out points around the base, and although this added a few extra grams, I was grateful for extra protection during that windy night in the mountains. Along with a new backpack and lighter clothing, I reduced my base weight to just over 7kg, greatly enhancing my enjoyment of walking on Skye (see Appendix 1 for my full kit list).

In a further effort to save weight, I decided to send half of my week's food rations ahead to Portree, located conveniently about halfway along my route. At first, I wondered if I could use an Amazon locker to facilitate this, but they only seem to be available for collecting items dispatched by Amazon. So instead, I phoned a smart-looking hotel I found on the internet (The Cuillin Hills) to ask if they would take in a package for me to collect at reception when passing. A friendly lady answered and immediately agreed to help, so I parcelled up the provisions in brown paper, along with a thank you note, and posted them Skyeward.

I was all set for an adventure on the misty isle.

3. OVER THE SEA TO SKYE

Day 1: Armadale to Ord, 12.7 miles

I padded down the gangplank of the ferry at Armadale on a blissful Wednesday morning. Three men from the crew stood around chatting on the slipway, occasionally breaking off their conversation to direct vehicles, mainly campervans, down the ramp. The eldest wore a red helmet, thick black glasses and a hi-vis jacket. He stood with hands on hips, conversing with a younger lad who was similarly dressed and maintained a respectful demeanour while resting one elbow on a wooden pallet converted into a planter, festooned with flowers. The unhurried conversation flowed in lilting tones with the occasional hand gesture or shrug over the riot of spiky purple flowers. I tried to imagine their topic of conversation at this idyllic jetty on the Sound of Sleat: tide times and football scores, local politics or distant wars?

Although it had taken me nearly 25 years to arrive at the start of *A Long Walk*, now I had landed I felt in

Ferry terminal at Armadale

no rush to set off. So instead, I ambled around the pier, taking in a large digital clock on the outside of the terminal office that displayed '08:10' and a sign that read, 'Welcome to Sleat, the garden of Skye' with the equivalent in Gaelic, *Fàilte gu Slèite, gàrragh an Eilein Sgitheanaich*. I suspected that 'gàrragh' means 'garden' in English and confirmed this later using Angus Watson's Gaelic-English Dictionary, although the word can also mean wall or enclosure. I looked around the tree-lined bay, and the word 'garden' did indeed seem like an appropriate epithet for this part of Skye, and I knew from studying the map that the first two days of my route would pass through several deciduous woods, a rarity on this *Eilein* of rock and grass.

I sat on a rock on the beach, taking in the environment: a robin sang from the undergrowth behind me; a pied wagtail scuttled across the sand; the sun rose over an assortment of small boats moored in the bay; there was a complete absence of wailing sirens that relentlessly drill my ears back home in the city. My soundtrack – or hummadruz – over the next seven days would be elemental.

I had long been anticipating the journey from Newcastle to Mallaig that I'd made the previous day. A fast train whizzed me up the Northumberland coast, past landmarks I'd become intimately acquainted with during my hike in 2019, such as the quaint village of Alnmouth overlooking its meandering estuary through which I waded to reach the far shore, and further north, Lindisfarne castle, that I'd sketched in my notebook from a peaceful bench overlooking Budle Bay. A rare moment of equanimity that summer. The train sped on over the Berwick viaduct and past coastal cliffs before depositing me at Waverley station in Edinburgh for a quick transfer to Glasgow Central. Arriving in Glasgow, I traversed the streets of Scotland's largest city to change stations under a dintless blue sky. The Duke of Wellington statue stood guard outside the Gallery of Modern Art, wearing a traffic cone on its head at a jaunty angle and holding another like a handbag. Naïve mosaics of colourful figures sparkled above from the portico. Small groups of young people lazed on the grass in George Square in front of the imposing City Chambers. Surrealism and sunshine were in the air.

I was unhorsed by a stuffy diesel train to Mallaig that vibrated hour after hour to mechanical Audenian rhythms: 'chug-chug, chug-chug; chug-chug, chug-chug'. The temperature rose and I slowly melted. There was no air-conditioning except for open windows, so I cooled my head with a wet flannel whilst standing in the corridor admiring the view. I passed the time identifying landmarks on the map: Loch Lomond flickered between the trees; the hills of Glen Coe rose above a baked Rannoch Moor; expiring walkers on the West Highland Way threw us a wave; miniature islands on Loch Eilt bristled with Scots pines like a display of Japanese bonsai.

As we rattled north, the railway line veered away from the road and went cross-country. The views were uncluttered by the usual signs of human infrastructure: a single thread of ballast, sleepers and steel, skimmed

Loch Eilt as seen from the train

thin across the landscape. If the train broke down in the expanse of Rannoch Moor, there would be no quick rescue or phone reception. I found this oddly thrilling, like a skier going off-piste or breaking an unwritten rule. I felt like I was doing something similar by backpacking across the Isle of Skye.

For me, backpacking is like passing through a mirror into another world: comforts are left behind, hardships are endured, and limits are tested; but ultimately, I gain a new sense of perspective, and senses are sharpened. With the single objective of walking day after day, my mind settles, and I inhabit my body. I feel like I'm living rather than just passing through. Raynor Winn described in *The Salt Path* that her husband Moth found something similar when walking the South West Coast Path after being diagnosed with a chronic disease. He defied the expectations of medics, and the disease was held at bay. To me, this seems perfectly natural: perpetual motion is our natural human state, what our species did for 95% of our time on this planet before the dawn of agriculture. Only in the last 10,000 years, and especially in the last 100 years, have we ceased constantly travelling about on foot – stravaiging, peregrinating, roaming, migrating – which is not sufficient time for our psychology and physiology to adapt.

*

I watched the waiting cars pull onto the ferry, and the ferrymen close the bow doors, then shouldered my pack and walked up the road – the first of many steps. I was aiming for the ruined village of Dalavil on the West coast of Sleat, about six miles to the northwest. I'd read Paterson's instructions in *A Long Walk* numerous times, and they had become totemic in my mind:

DAY ONE, AM ARMADALE PIER TO DALAVIL (8.5kms, ½ day, height-gain 230m): Follow the road out of the carpark at the pier and take a left fork signposted Ardvasar. Walk through the village past the shop and post-office, and turn right at the old police-station, going steeply uphill for two hundred metres to fork left through a gate beside a bungalow. Follow the track through another gate onto the open hillside. Continue up open slopes towards the skyline to the north, heading for a bealach between two low rounded hills…

I'd read the words, studied the route on the map, and probably dreamt of them, but half an hour later, I found myself above the village in a field with a nervous-looking horse for company and no obvious way ahead. A portentous start? I've always found navigating the first mile of a journey the most difficult, especially when leaving a town – excitement, getting my bearings, narrow vistas – and after several hiking misadventures with farm animals, I eyed the horse warily and gave it a wide berth. At the top of the field was a building site where several workmen were constructing a Scandi-style house of wood and glass, and beyond lay the track leading to the open hillside described by Paterson. I wondered if the newbuild had blocked Paterson's original route. I hailed one of the men through a temporary palisade fence and asked if I could cross. Permission was granted, and a degree of equanimity was restored to the mind of the protagonist.

It wasn't long before I found my stride and crested the brow of the hills separating the peninsula's east and west coast. Jumping over a small stream, I startled a snipe that buzzed off erratically, zig-zag fashion, as if trying to avoid a shotgun. It was the first of half a dozen such birds I would nearly tread on traversing Sleat, always appearing unexpectedly. And despite the abundance of such birds, now I think back on it, I don't recall seeing a single grouse butt or mammal trap on Skye, like those that litter the North Pennines. When walking alone, my mood is affected by such signs as if I'm an ecological weathervane. I love diversity and wouldn't be disappointed by the riches ahead.

Behind me, the sun was now high in the sky over the Sound of Sleat, where the ferry was still visible – plying its trade over the shimmering sea to Skye. Ahead, on a distant horizon, a ridge of serrated, spiky, menacing peaks reached for the sky like nothing I'd seen in northern England. I checked the compass bearing against my map and discovered I'd already caught sight of the famous Cuillin Hills. I was transfixed. I learned on a BBC Radio 4 broadcast that the word 'Cuillin' is thought to either derive from the Gaelic for 'holly' or Old Norse for 'keel of a boat', but after studying the profile, my instinct tells me it is the latter. The programme was presented by writer Robert Macfarlane, who attempted a continuous traverse of the precipitous Cuillin ridge over two days, bivouacking half way. I would be circumnavigating those mountains, but a few days later, when walking down the shore of Loch Slapin, I had plenty of time to observe the Cuillins' profile and studied their shape from left to right: backwards-facing nose; horse's saddle; chameleon's head, back and tail; volcano; dragon's wings... and so on.

To the right of The Cuillins, set apart and slightly closer, was a second mountain, triangular in shape, that I thought to be Blà Bheinn, also written Blaven. Before departing, I had consulted my father, who has climbed all the Munros, about the possibility of tackling Blaven as a diversion from my route, but in the end, it turned out to be beyond my abilities with a backpack, especially considering the time it would take me to cross Sleat.

I descended from the ridge bumbling over uneven ground flecked with purple heather until a long and gentle valley came into view, drained by a meandering tree-lined river running into a shallow loch: Loch a' Ghlinne (Loch of the Glen). A spindly rowan tree with silver bark framed the scene to my left, while the hills on the valley's far side were clothed with lush, broadleaved trees.

Loch a' Ghlinne in Gleann Meadhonach

At the bottom of the slope, near the river, I climbed over a wire fence and paused to drink. The slumbering glen basked in the warm, still air as if it sought to absorb as much heat as possible before the winter ahead. Already, I felt a sense of isolation, cocooned in this middle glen; not a road or building in sight. The only sweet airs were the occasional 'peep' of a meadow pipit and the river cascading over rocks.

Across the river, I joined my first good path since Armadale, which led past a ruin that would once have been a substantial home, but now trees thrust upwards between the tumbled stones. A reminder that this deserted valley would once have been home to a community of crofters, making a living from the land and sea. Everywhere Tracy and I have visited on the west coast of Scotland, from Ardnamurchan to Mull, we've seen similar abandoned villages, and the story is always the same: powerful landowners clearing the land of indigenous people for their own selfish gain. Such scenes add a mournful tone to the landscape, but at least the country has learned from such atrocities, and two centuries later, there are signs of restoration. On some Scottish islands, such as Ulva, communities have taken control of their destiny following Scotland's Land Reform Act of 2003 by buying back the land. And the new laws also introduced a right to roam – and camp – responsibly in the wild. One day, I hope that similar reforms will be made where I live in Northumberland, freeing the soul.

I continued along the path towards the wood I had spotted earlier. The forested area was encircled by a high fence, and on the gate, a sign announced, 'Collie Dalavil, Site of Special Scientific Interest'. A second, weather-beaten poster explained that the land belongs to The Clan Donald Lands Trust and the fence is to exclude sheep and deer, allowing seedlings to regenerate in the wood, which is of particular interest for ancient woodland, peatland, dragonflies and lichen. The Trust was formed following a community buyout in 1971 following the death of the clan chief, Alexander Macdonald, even before the Land Reform Act.

Through the gate, I discovered that Dalavil Forest is indeed worth protecting. The ground jumped with toads, holly sprouted from fallen branches, spiders webbed the path; the mythologically-named grass of Parnassus, with its sophisticated white petals laced with green, adorned the verge; abundant blackberries offered a mobile feast; dragonflies hawked their territories, like jewelled antediluvian wardens.

I meandered between tall trees – which occasionally framed views of the lily-pad-covered loch – as if they'd been deliberately positioned for aesthetic appeal, and then I remembered the monicker for Sleat: 'The Garden of Skye'. I found the forest so delightful that I invented reasons to linger, especially as I knew the temperature would soar on emerging from its protective shade, so I sat down and sketched a skyrocketing beech tree in my notebook.

I tore myself away from the woodland charms just after midday with thoughts of lunch. In *A Long Walk,* Paterson described and photographed a stone bothy with a tin roof standing to the side of the track between the forest and coast where he rested in 1998, but the intervening quarter-of-a-century has not been kind to the shelter. I found it roofless, the corrugated iron casually discarded to one side, presumably torn off in a gale. Through a vacant, deep-set window, I saw a clay chimney top, collapsed inside, around which miniature ferns sprouted profusely from every crack. So, I walked to the end of the track where the river, flowing from the lily pad loch, emerged into a small estuary.

I was just thinking this would be an excellent place for lunch and scan for otters slithering amongst the rocks when, at the end of the path, I came across a party of four young women, clad in boots and hiking gear, sitting on rocks eating sandwiches; the first people I'd seen since leaving Armadale. We chatted briefly about our routes and abundance of toads, but I didn't want to disturb them, so pushed on beyond the end of the path. I then found myself in a fractured landscape of shattered rocks and waist-high bracken that concealed ankle-breaking traps. Paterson (himself a seasoned mountaineer) describes this section of the coast as arduous, 'The bigger streams have carved deep gullies through the slopes above the clifftops, and there is many a scramble in and out of these', but he doesn't mention the feature that called to me like a beacon: an isthmus of pure white sand stretching out to sea between rocks and seaweed: a Caribbean mirage. Tracy will tell you, it's rare anything comes between me and food, but the prospect of a swim over white sand to cool off before lunch was a strong lure, so I negotiated the rugged terrain for another half an hour to reach my new goal.

The water was as clear as clear could be, and I could see my shadow mirroring the movement of my arms and legs on the sand below. I wished I'd brought my goggles because I might have spied an aquarium of fish inhabiting their secret world. I drifted on my front between rocks and fronds of bladderwrack, searching for crabs and blood-red anemones, but discovered I could see through the water best by standing up in the shallows and looking down. I sometimes go snorkelling in the summer off the coast of Northumberland, but the water's murky by comparison.

Feeling refreshed, I dried off before munching my overdue lunch to the sound of my stove boiling water for a cup of tea. As my footprints on the soft sand were slowly swept away by the water, I scanned the horizon from left to right: the hills of Rùm gently dropped down to the sea before the Cuillins abruptly rose to a crenelation of summits, with saucer-like clouds drifting above. A scene from a glossy holiday brochure.

As I was packing up my stove, a sea kayak rounded the isthmus and entered the small bay where I swam. I waved to the paddler, who returned the gesture and commented on the excellent weather before moving on, effortlessly gliding around the coastline. By contrast, it took me an hour and a half to reach the road to Tarskavaig. However, the slow going was compensated for by stumbling across an adder snaking its way under the grass along the edge of a bog. Adders are my Holy Grail of British wildlife, and

Beach on the west coast of Sleat with Cuillin Hills on the skyline

I've walked for weeks in The Cheviots without seeing one, despite regularly admiring pictures of them on social media. I guess this is either because I've got my head in the clouds looking for birds or, as Tracy might say with a grin, I am 'heavy-footed'!

Nevertheless, my third-ever wild adder was a fine specimen: almost gold in colour with characteristic black diamonds zigzagging down its long back and tail, effortlessly camouflaged against the rusty leaves and black peat. As soon as it spotted me, it froze, regarding me through peeled brown eyes, head kinked to one side: pensive, patient, imperious, poikilothermic.

I find the idea of snakes, especially poisonous snakes, delightfully subversive in ecologically sanitised Britain. So far, at least, adders have escaped the fate of other once native 'dangerous' animals, such as bears, wolves, lynx… and now badgers. I probably would have been no less surprised to stumble across a walrus.

*

It was a welcome mental and physical release to step off the heather and onto the tarmacked road to Ord – I raised my head and enjoyed the twittering of birds in the trees and regarded rowan berries glowing in the afternoon light. With the sun behind me, all the colours were saturated: deep blue sky, bright red berries, glossy green leaves.

When the village of Tarskavaig appeared on my left – a panorama of scattered white houses sitting pretty on an undulating hillside, with the Cuillin Hills looming beyond

– I matched it from memory to the cover photograph of Paterson's *A Long Walk*. I spent a few minutes attempting to replicate the photo on my camera phone, but comparing the images now, I must have got the viewpoint wonky, or a house has been built in the foreground since. Paterson's lines lead, whereas mine are lost.

Paterson writes that once Tarskavaig was a 'clearance village' where evicted islanders were resettled, but now it is inhabited mainly by retired folk and the occasional newcomer. He also warns that there are no shops or facilities in any of Sleat's west coast villages, and all supplies must be shipped a twenty-five-kilometre round-trip from Ardvasar along the narrow, switchback road. Fortunately, I was carrying sufficient supplies to reach Portree, or at least that's what I hoped.

Down the hill from Tarskavaig a wide bay opened out to my left and there was a handwritten sign on a slate: 'FOOTPATH TO CASTLE'. An open gate led to a track, at the end of which rose a hulk of rock guarding the right arm of the bay connected to the land by a dilapidated stone arch. It would have been temping to investigate what was marked on my map as the remains of Dùn Scaich Castle, but time was getting the better of me, so I left it for a future visit.

*

After a few more miles on the tree-lined road, an unusually small signpost announced my arrival in Ord, surely a contender for the shortest Gaelic place name.

Intrigued by the sign, I later investigated its meaning: the *Isleofskye.com* website says that Ord means 'Rounded Hill', but this definition doesn't seem to match the terrain as the village is perched on the hillside overlooking a rocky bay. By contrast, Watson's Gaelic Dictionary translates òrd as 'hammer', and the Sleat Local History Society website says that in Old Norse 'urd' is a heap of boulders at the foot of a steep face; 'vord' is a beacon hill; and àrd is 'high' or a 'height'. All contenders.

Further digging revealed that Scottish poet Alexander Smith stayed in Ord at his father-in-law's house in the 1860s, where he was inspired to write a book, *A Summer in Skye*. Surely, he mentioned its derivation... I was soon swept up in Smith's sagacious descriptions of the landscape, people and culture he encountered. In those days, Skye was full of activity: crofters inhabited smoky turf huts, tended their crops and gathered shellfish on the shore; shepherds drove sheep and cattle to market in Broadford where deals were settled over jugs of whisky; gillies hunted anything that moved – otters, polecats, deer, eagles – with dogs and guns; tourists flocked from across Europe to marvel at Glen Sligachan and the Quiraing, arriving on steamers. Nearly everyone Smith met conversed in Gaelic, could sing and dance, and was superstitious. Some were said to have second sight. The landscape was soaked in legends of fairies, giants and castles. People found meaning in *place* – bordering on animism. And yet, Smith also observed the horror of the highland clearances first hand, with landlords tearing down houses and deporting entire glens to Canada. In the end, Smith never mentioned the true meaning of 'Ord', but I was transported in time and place in the way only a good travelogue can.

*

Back in present day Ord, a grey-haired lady – probably a grandmother – wearing a purple pleated daisy-print top, sat on a bench overlooking the bay, serenely taking photos of a family in the water: two swimming and two kayaking; a scene reminiscent of a Ladybird book cover illustrating a day out at the seaside.

Beyond this idyll, on the far side of the loch, a black cliff rose abruptly from the water, an obstacle I would reach in a day or two's time. Behind me, the sun slouched lower in the sky, casting crepuscular rays over the sea, doing his 'very best to make the billows smooth and white' in the words of my favourite poem by Lewis Carroll that are my companion on every walk. The light display tempted a couple into the garden of their holiday cottage, where they stood beside a whirly-gig washing line, taking photos.

Sensing I wouldn't get much further before nightfall, I knocked on the door of the last house in the village and asked the man who answered if he would kindly fill my water bottles, explaining I was hiking across Skye. He obliged and disappeared inside with my empty bottles. I waited at the door like I've done many times before on long hikes, feeling grateful for the kindness of strangers and – in that no-man's-land between asking and receiving – wondering how adequately to express my gratitude.

Earlier that year, in March, when there was still snow in the air, I had backpacked through the New Forest from near Salisbury to Lymington where my grandparents once lived, to immerse myself in childhood memories of England's savanna. Redwings flocked, kites drifted, starlings chattered, deer barked. Near the end of my journey, I knocked on the door of a bungalow for water. An elderly lady answered, who brewed me a cup of tea and told me her life's story through the living room window while I sat on a chair outside. It was too cold for her to come out, and I was too conscientious to go in, having spent several nights in my tent. Apart from her name, Mary, the details of our conversations have escaped me because earlier that day, whilst walking through the heart of the Forest, I received a phone call from Tracy telling me that my only cousin, Stephen, whom I grew up with in Nottingham, had died suddenly of a heart attack. I felt numb. Shock. Disbelief. Empty. Lonely. Cold. The only place I wanted to be was with my auntie in Nottingham. I didn't tell Mary this tragic news, but it was as if she had been sent to comfort me.

*

When the man returned with my full bottles, I sensed he was local, so I asked about the way ahead: 'Have you ever walked from here to Heaste, around the loch?'

'No, I've never walked that far. There is a path up to the old house – about a mile – but beyond that, I think you might struggle to get around.' I thanked him and

(Top): Tarskavaig with the Cuillin Hills on the skyline
(Bottom): Ord beach

turned to leave, considering the implications of his advice. Then I heard a voice calling after me: 'If you *are* hoping to get to Heaste, you'll need that!' I turned around and saw the man pointing towards my map, lying on the gravel. With more thanks and a little embarrassment, I crunched down the drive.

The house the Ordonian referred to was a large, square stone building set back from a broad, isolated bay with a view of the Cuillins beyond, and now, I wonder if it was the same building in which Smith stayed in 1864. He described the Cuillins as 'jagged and notched like an old sword-blade'. To my delight, there was a flat grassy area between the house and the bay with a stream running through it; it would be difficult to conceive of a better place to camp on my first night, especially as I needed practice pitching my new tent. But first, I thought it best to investigate the house and ask for permission to camp if it was inhabited. Fortunately, no one was home, and the place looked like a building site with scaffolding around one side and dozens of paint tins stacked in a dilapidated kitchen. So, I returned to the grass and lavished my full attention on unpacking my bags and pitching my tent. I'd done a couple of practice pitches, once in my local park and then when staying at a holiday cottage, but not having a garden at home, such opportunities are limited.

Every wild campsite is different – slope, surface, exposure, vegetation – but as I'd hoped, it went up with no bother according to the instructions: unroll on the ground; insert four pegs around the base; insert two trekking poles extended to 120cm; peg out two guy ropes.

The inner was already attached to the outer, and no fiddly bits like pushing tiny poles through seams like on my other tent. Less time crouching on the floor means less pain in my back.

As the sun sank behind the hills to the west, I washed in the stream before boiling water on my stove to rehydrate my freeze-dried meal. This time, I remembered to remove the silica gel sachet and not sprinkle it over the food, mistakenly thinking it was salt – a possible cause of my food poisoning incident in Northumberland! I carried my sit-mat, meal and long-handled spoon to the shoreline and then rested on a rock, conveniently low.

After dinner, I crawled into my tent and zipped up the inner, just as the midges rose. I bedded down for the night reading *The Stand* on my Kindle. The only thing bothering me was not getting any phone reception since I had left Armadale to update Tracy on my progress.

4. SLEAT'S LABYRINTH

Day 2: Ord to Heaste, 8.8 miles

Despite finding the perfect pitch, being warm, dry and level, and stuffing all my spare clothes into a dry bag to make a large, comfortable pillow, I woke with a splitting headache. This wasn't unexpected, as I've had it before when camping, so I took some painkillers, drank water, and tried to concentrate on the soft glow of the sunrise reflecting on the distant hills across the water. Although my view was obscured by the fly screen, much to the chagrin of a thousand hungry midges gathered around my tent, I caught the unmistakable profile of an otter slithering through the glassy water. I grabbed my binoculars and had time to get a close-up before it melted into the loch: fur, whiskers, tail, gone.

While eating breakfast, I watched a young couple walk down to the bay from a cliff on the far side. She sat on a rock while he changed into a wetsuit and went for a swim. I hatched a plan to ask them if they could get a phone signal to send a message to Tracy, so I delayed my departure until

Morning at first campsite north of Ord

he was back on dry land, changed, and then walked over to them. 'Hello,' I called, still some way off so as not to startle them. 'A beautiful morning for a swim.'

'Yes, it's great weather for this time of year,' he replied.

'Did you see an otter when you were in the water? I spotted one from my tent earlier.'

He shook his head. 'No, but the water was clear; I'll look out for it.'

His partner added, 'We were camping up there, with a view of Coral Island–' she pointed behind her– 'but we're staying with my aunty in Ord; I'll tell her you saw an otter when we return. She'll be pleased to know; she told us she saw a white-tailed eagle flying up the loch a few days ago.'

I commented on how lucky they were to have a relative living in such a beautiful place, 'a free Airbnb' and then asked if she would mind sending a message to my wife when they got back to the house to tell her where I was. She enthusiastically rose to the task and insisted on photographing me on her phone to accompany the message. I stood there – slightly perplexed, wondering how Tracy would feel when she received a text message from this helpful stranger – while she took a couple of snaps. I wrote Tracy's number for her on a torn-out page from my notebook before thanking them and heading up the cliff in the direction they'd camped.

I climbed the narrow gully up to their crow's nest of a camping spot with a fine view over the loch. A few hundred yards out was a white sandy island with a few black jagged rocks, which, I supposed, must be the Coral

Island. My imagination filled in the details: pirate ship, buried treasure, emeralds and rubies.

*

Eventually, my path would take me north to the mountains in Central Skye, but before then, I had to circumnavigate Loch Eishort. Although, on the map, Ord to Boreraig (an abandoned township directly opposite on the north shore) is only 11 miles, if I knew then what I know now, I would have chartered a fishing boat to traverse the much shorter distance across the water, like Smith and his host did in *A Summer on Skye* on a day trip to Loch Coruisk from Ord.

Stepping away from the campsite, I descended into a vegetative malaise of waist-deep bracken, heather and bilberry bushes, shrouding a landscape of cliffs and gullies that seemed designed by a malevolent force to block my progress. It would take me nine hours to cover as many miles, although I probably walked much further, meandering and backtracking. Paterson warns of the problematic terrain:

> The beach is rocky and uneven, and the walking is hard. When the tide is up, the shore is covered virtually to ·the treeline, and the walker must make use of the frequent heavily-wooded slopes above.

It must have been high tide because I found the shoreline impassable, with sea cliffs blocking the route. The terrain had agency, pushing me higher and higher up the hillside, controlling my steps, until after several hours, I found myself in an extensive forest of wind-blown birch. My progress through the wood was made a little easier because it was grassy underfoot, probably nibbled by sheep, but I was always on a steep camber, and my feet slouched painfully to the side of my boots. I paused to catch my breath and looked around: twisted silvery trunks sprouted at odd angles from the mossy floor, more often horizontal than vertical; crusting lichen peppered with red spots jewelled the trunks; cascades of hanging lichen bedecked gangly branches like Halloween decorations; spiders webbed every gap. I came eye to eye with a fly lovingly cocooned in a silk coffin, pondering its fate. All was eerily quiet except for a stream burbling down the steep slope.

I'd recently read *The Lost Rainforests of Britain* by Guy Shrubsole and wondered if this was on his list. 'A temperate rainforest', Shrubsole writes, 'is wood where it's wet and mild enough for plants to grow on other plants', a habitat rarer than tropical rainforest covering just one per cent of the world's surface and less than 0.5 per cent of Britain. The author is a studious researcher and cartophile, and illustrates the regions of the UK that are sufficiently wet to support rainforest habitat alongside a map of ancient woodland fragments (in Scotland, those in continuous existence since 1750). Unsurprisingly, these potential rainforests – many of which he visited

Birch woods on Sleat

when writing the book – lie along the western coast of England, Wales, and Scotland. Examining the book now, with the aid of a magnifying glass, I can just about discern five patches of green on the Isle of Skye, four on Sleat and one just around the corner near Torrin. Also, the whole of Skye is firmly within the 'hyper-oceanic' climatic zone, benefiting from high levels of rainfall and *supposedly* cool summers. And, one of those green dots does indeed sit on the north coast of Sleat where I was admiring the lichen. Shrubsole didn't visit Skye when researching his book, but he was wowed by fragments of rainforest around Fort William, and in particular, 'The hanging gardens of Glasdrum' on the north shore of Loch Creran where he revelled in a drenched alien world of lichens and bryophytes, including a treacle-like fungus that feeds on dead hazel by catching branches as they fall, suspending animation. He also commented on the remarkable circularity of wet woods 'with fallen branches sprouting fresh twigs' and providing shelter to saplings, or 'phoenix trees', in the words of his guide. A complex, three-dimensional, functioning ecosystem that is so rare in the UK.

A decade ago, Tracy and I were fortunate enough to visit a tropical rainforest in Uganda, where we had the transformational experience of seeing a family of mountain gorillas interacting in the wild. Since then, I occasionally feel bereft when exploring supposedly wild places in the UK due to their lack of diversity, and my overall impression from reading *The Lost Rainforests* was like that of an Ent in *Lord of the Rings* who thought he was the last of his species only to discover a few hardy magical souls hanging on into The Fourth Age: The Age of Men. But is there any hope of recovery?

Shrubsole concludes that, like elsewhere in the UK, the outlook for Scotland's rainforest hangs in the balance, with only around 74,000 acres remaining, and most of those failing to rejuvenate due to the relentless grazing pressures of deer and sheep. 'Veteran trees stand stricken and lonely on barren hillsides that used to be forest, watching their remaining companions collapse into senescence.' But there is hope: NatureScot has new powers to cull deer where they are getting out of control following a report published by the independent Deer Working Group in 2020, and some rainforest fragments have been saved and restored by local communities with help from Scotland's Community Right to Buy legislation. In an amusing anecdote combining modern Scottish politics with ancient etymology, Shrubsole describes an online argument between a Gaelic Twitter account and the Scottish Green Party in 2021 after the latter mentioned the *rainforests* on Scotland's west coast, a statement ridiculed by the former as *craicte* (crazy). 'But the tweet ended up getting ratioed with a string of responses from Gaelic and English speakers alike – pointing out that, actually, Scotland *does* have rainforest; that it's a recognised habitat, not some mythical invention; and that it's something many in Scotland feel justifiably proud about.' Shrubsole signs off Chapter 9, 'Forest People', revealing 'that the term 'Gaelic' itself derives from a word meaning 'forest people'', and The

Highland Clearances not only robbed the Gaels of their land but also their identity by stripping the once forested landscape bare.

Happily for me, back in Sleat, the land was not bare; in fact, if anything, the wood became thicker as I pushed eastwards until the ground ahead dropped at an alarming angle until it became a sheer drop of around 20 feet into a dark narrow gully, the far side of which – at eye level – seemed tantalisingly close. For maybe 20 or 30 minutes, I scouted uphill and downhill, searching for a safe place to cross, but bracken and spiky branches blocked my path. Perhaps unwisely, I took the advice of my rugby teacher at school, who used to yell up the pitch: 'One yard forward is better than 20 yards sideways', and so committed to the muddy cliff ahead – half climbing and half sliding. I grabbed at the slope for purchase, but tufts of moss came away in my hand. I landed with a splash in the dark water at the bottom to find myself in a Jurassic world of ferns, ivy and fallen trees dangling from overhanging rocks. Up the gorge, a narrow waterspout cascaded from a V in the rocks into a small plunge pool. As I studied the moss-covered cliff face ahead, it crossed my mind that I was in a degree of jeopardy: at the bottom of a deep gully, miles from civilisation, no phone reception. A sudden thunderstorm could be fatal, washing me away like a cork. I wondered who, if anyone, had last set foot in this green womb, the heart of the labyrinth.

It was as if I was reliving a book by David Mitchell, *The Bone Clocks*, in which Holly Sykes is trapped in a collapsing labyrinth designed by a band of child-sacrificing

Eternals known as Anchorites. She only escapes because she memorises a map drawn by her possessed brother, Jacko, allowing her to reach the maze's centre and grasp a portal in the form of a golden apple. A rolling pin also came in handy to disable one of the ringleaders. Perhaps I should have heeded Mitchell's lesson and better memorised my map.

Climbing upwards was out of the question unless I grew suckers on my hands and feet, so I took the only other option – slither downstream until an escape route presented itself. I squeezed between two rocks before dropping about six feet over the ledge of another waterfall. After negotiating the edge of the plunge pool, I saw what could optimistically be described as a narrow ledge angling steeply upwards on the far bank. Again, the handholds were no better than clods of sodden earth, but somehow, I made it to the top with the aid of a few firmly rooted bushes. I grabbed a small tree trunk to steady myself and craned my neck toward the steeply rising slope ahead, only to be met by the bewildered gaze of five horned sheep high above on the brow of the hill, backed by a startlingly blue sky: the welcoming committee. I'm sure I heard one say to the other, 'the last eejit came this way in 1998, and look what happened to him'!

A little further on, I encountered yet another deep gully of similar proportions, where I fell on my knees and cried for the lack of progress – *my kingdom, my kingdom for a path* – but this time, I climbed uphill to the source rather than risking a fall.

Soon after, my progress was blocked for a third time by a man-made obstacle: a ten-foot-high deer fence that stretched across the horizon – the first of three such fences I would cross over the next two days. I paused to consider my approach: I walked up and down, looking for a crossing point, and noticed a taller, stouter post; I took off my backpack and hurled it over like a shot-putter – it was assured of a soft landing due to the heather, bog and moss. My poles followed the backpack, leaving me to climb the wire ladder using the post for stability.

I was hot, sweaty and tired but finally ascended to the crest of a ridge, where, at last, I got a view towards the head of the loch. I had escaped the labyrinth of Sleat with just a few scratches. I sat down amongst the deep heather on a rock with a small tree for shade above. The sun was high, and suddenly, the air was alive with insects. They attack when you stop. But these weren't midges; they were tiny black robotic drones with six angled legs and a flat, stiff back. They landed on my skin, then crawled in stealth mode to hide. I know this for sure because that night, I found one dead inside my pants. What it died of, I can only imagine. Keds: blood-sucking flies that inhabit a host for life after shedding their wings, like a pet vampire.

I ferreted in my backpack for lunch. Somewhere back in the wilderness, I must have dropped my bag of nuts, so that just left me with cheese and salami wraps. I had packed rations to last for three days to reach Portree:

Crossing a gully on Sleat

three freeze-dried dinners, three bags of cereal premixed with milk powder, and three lunches – two of each were left. The nuts were for snacks. Sitting on that hot, remote hillside, I discovered, to my dismay, that my cheese and salami were on the verge of going rancid – probably cooked on the train to Mallaig. I considered heating up one of my two remaining dinners but knew that would leave me short, so peeled off several layers of sweaty cheese into a wrap. I didn't risk the meat.

As I ate, I took stock of the landscape ahead. The head of the loch was flatter, and the beach broader, so after lunch, I gave up on the hillside and descended a tricky slope to the water's edge, crossing another deer fence. Although rocks on the shore were like oversized railway ballast, and I had to watch every step to avoid twisting an ankle, it was a welcome change from what had gone before. It was an ideal habitat for otters, but I stood no chance of seeing another, with the constant crunch of feet and clack of poles over the cobble-wobblers.

At around 3pm, I found a welcome oak tree perched on the shoreline, offering a protective dome of shade. After a restorative dip in the water, carefully avoiding a beached jellyfish, I stretched out my towel to dry, lay back and relaxed. I felt like putting down roots there for the rest of the day, just chilling out. All I could hear was a small boat chugging up and down to a shellfish farm in the middle of the loch. Above me were leaves of green and sky of blue. Simple pleasures. Before moving on, I sat on a large red buoy that someone had tied to the oak, put my head back, kicked my legs, and swung.

Finally, I reached the head of Loch Eishort, where there is a delta. Although Paterson warns against crossing here due to deep mud, I jumped across a few gravelly streams. Near the middle of the delta, I stood and watched the river unbraid into multiple channels before joining the loch. The distinction between land and water, erosion and deposition, uncertain. A place where ever-shifting edges overwrite yesterday's patterns. Shapes formed and reformed: the end of a frayed rope, a harp, a trident. It's exhilarating to watch natural processes left to play their games, untamed by dams, levees, or abstraction. Not only are deltas beautiful, they also are biodiversity hot spots and protect coastal communities from hurricanes and flooding – acting like a giant sponge.

I ask myself if I'm more like a natural delta or a canalised river: home, work, leisure? Tracy would say that I like routine, and she's probably right. But I also know that without allowing change my brain will fossilise. The death of my cousin made me want to shutter myself up, and catch life by the tail, in equal measure. Take my morning walk, reassuringly familiar for the last 13 years, but I push myself to notice the details: the smile of the women in the laundrette, the crocheted Christmas tree on the post box, the hedge of chirping sparrows, pigeons swanning around the church tower. But I do, very nearly always, *walk*. Each morning, yearning to feel the changing seasons, the sparrows building nests, the crocheted Christmas tree becoming an Easter egg, the woman still smiling. The antidote to the groove becoming deeper is to have transient boundaries, like

Oak tree on Loch Eishort (a welcome break)

the shifting delta: take a different route or even the same route in reverse. Walking across Skye was partly about challenging myself to take a new path.

I continued to stand in the middle of the delta and watch the water: the streams appeared to flow uphill into the loch as if the law of gravity was reversed. Then, a little grebe flapped its tiny wings and ran across the water, attempting to fly.

*

I crossed the river, Abhainn Ceann Loch Eishort (The River at the Head of the Loch), just after 4pm, where it was just possible to leap across several rocks to reach the far bank without getting wet feet. I then wobbled back along the north side of the loch, determined to stick to the shore, no matter how uneven underfoot. It clouded over, giving some relief from the sun, and I paused at a stream to filter water and refill my bottles. Despite the heat, my headache had cleared, I suspect due to the electrolyte tablets Tracy had given me to put in my water. It was the first time I'd used them on a walk, and I enjoyed the mildly strawberry-tasting water and watching them fizz in the bottle like a soda stream.

Whilst I was filtering, I gazed across the loch and saw the oak tree on the opposite shore where I'd stopped earlier, and then noticed several seals that I supposed were fishing for the mussels or oysters growing in the floating farm. They poked their noses up inquisitively as if to say hello but vanished at the first sign of movement.

As the closest living relative I'd met since leaving Ord, I welcomed their company and wondered if they would sing their mournful Selkie chorus, like the ones that had enchanted Tracy and me on the Lindisfarne causeway earlier that year, hundreds strong. I once heard about someone who could sing in the language of seals, so, given the total isolation, I tried to mimic their sound, but it had no effect.

Slowing to search for water on a long walk brings me closer to nature and makes me think about the lie of the land, its history, and who might have lived there. The next day, I would fill my bottles from a stream that flowed through the ruined village of Boreraig, which would have been its lifeblood, cascading down from the hillside, winding around the stone dwellings. When walking in Northumberland, I drank from a stream on the coast at Howick, a place where there was once a roundhouse built by some of the first stone-age settlers to the region ten thousand years ago; also, from a stream at Chew Green in The Cheviots, where Roman invaders built a forward camp on a lonely hillside, north of their protective wall. Waterways are the confluence of geography and history.

After clambering over a tricky section of the coastline that was half-thinking about becoming a cliff, I rounded a bend to see a broad bay home to a few boats, faced by houses stretching up the hill behind: the hamlet of Heaste. Except for a car and trailer parked at the end of the beach and a stack of pallets and wood piled up on the grass as if for a bonfire, the village seemed deserted.

Tired as I was, I considered knocking on a door to ask if I could pay a few pounds to camp in someone's garden or field, but after such a taciturn day, the imposition jarred, so I followed a muddy track through the village and over the brow of a small hill beyond which the land dipped down again to the shore where there was a cattle trough and sheep pen. From the map, I could see this was the last flattish area to camp before the track climbed steeply uphill. But cow pats were everywhere, and marauding cows a potential danger.

With little energy left and unwilling to return to the village, I walked down to the shore, where there was a salt marsh covered in short grass like a golf course. Between the islands of grass deep gullies had been carved by the ebb and flow of the tide. It was the perfect spot unless there was a high tide. I inspected the tallest grassy island and noticed it was ringed by a tideline of seaweed a few feet from the edge, sparing a higher, drier patch in the middle. Over the loch, a half-moon, not a full moon, had risen, which I thought was a good omen. So, with great relief after the long day and some anxiety, I made my camp for the night in this salty dell or *fideach*.

After pitching my tent and having dinner, I repacked all my loose belongings back into dry bags in case of flood, and read a few more pages of *The Stand* on my Kindle:

Now take away all his books, all his friends, and his stereo. Also remove all sustenance except what he can glean along the way. It's an emptying-out process and also a diminishing of the ego. Your selves, gentlemen—they are turning into a window-glass. Or better yet, empty tumblers." "But what's the point?" Ralph asked. "Why go through all the rigmarole?"' – and fell into an uneasy sleep.

Second campsite near Heast

5. MUNIFICENCE IN TORRIN

Day 3: Heaste to Bealach na Bèiste, 9 miles

I woke several times during the night to peer out of my tent, trying to slice the darkness with my torch to discern if the inky black water was creeping closer. At one point, I might have been marooned, but come the morning, it was clear my bet had paid off. Relief: if my down sleeping bag had got wet, it would have been game over.

Despite clouds of midges, I made a good start and was on my way by 7am, climbing up a track – yes, an actual path – away from Heaste. When scouting the route from Heaste to Boreraig for *A Long Walk*, at first Paterson tried the coast, which he found was rough and pathless, but then villagers told him of an ancient track that doesn't appear on modern maps that runs inland, over the hills. I hoped I was on that track, but there was no way to be sure: I only had Paterson's description, 'A flagstone footbridge crosses the stream, and a sketchy path then leads into and through the trees'.

Halfway up the slope, with my head still covered with a midge net, I stopped to watch the sun rise over mountains to the east, tinting the still waters of Loch Eishort peachy orange, highlighting a striped pattern of ridge and furrows on a field below. The village of Heaste lay dormant, stretched out along a winding road. Ahead, the hillside was transformed into a palette of sage green and hot purple.

Paterson's description of the journey from Heaste to Boreraig reads like a hop, skip and a jump, but it took me over two hours to cover the two-and-a-bit miles. At the top of the hill, the ancient track dissolved into a bog, which morphed into waist-deep vegetation hiding pothole-like man traps: déjà vu. I lost a leg in one furrow nearly up to my waist. If it hadn't been for the assistance of my trekking poles, I'm sure I would have twisted an ankle. However, after climbing another deer fence, I found myself at the top of a cliff with a stunning view of the mouth of Loch Eishort: dramatic cliffs rose from the water's edge on the near side, the meandering coastline of Coral Island and Ord lay on the far side, volcanic Rùm dominated the skyline. Far below me lay a white pebble beach ringed with three tide lines of seaweed. The beach swept around to a rocky peninsula that pointed directly towards an island in the middle of the loch: Eilean Gaineamhach Boreraig. As I've been writing about Skye, I've been keeping a note of the Gaelic landmarks I passed, doing my best to translate them and memorise some words to add a layer of meaning to future trips. 'Eilean' means island; 'Gaineamhach' or

'Gainmheach' means sand; and Boreraig is the place, meaning unknown: thus, Sandy Island of Boreraig.

Except for the plastic fishing debris, the beach was enchanting. Out in the loch, a family of mergansers dived for fish, ravens croaked from the cliffs above, and pipits fed on insects amongst the tide wrack. In places, white pebbles gave way to smooth grey rocks that rose like an archipelago of miniature islands above a cloud inversion. At the end of the bay, a waterfall of brilliant white fell almost vertically over a cliff into a plunge pool on the beach around 30 feet below. The cliff was flanked by tall rowan trees festooned in red berries, around which grew ferns and ivy. I could have easily spent a day here, in which case I might have discovered the rich seam of fossils Paterson found on the cliff behind the waterfall during his visit.

Up in Boreraig above the waterfall was a grassy clearing surrounded by tumbledown cottages gradually succumbing to the effects of gravity, time and nature. Paterson was entranced by this place and wrote:

The remains have an atmosphere at once poignant and powerful, and all kinds of equivalents spring immediately to mind - the ancient ruined cities of the Turkish Mediterranean, Macchu Picchu (in the glen instead of the mountain-top) and other vanished peoples and lost civilisations. And that, of course, is exactly what these ruins represent - the lost civilisation of Gael.

Looking west down Loch Eishort with Rùm on the horizon

Paterson picked brambles and green hazelnuts for lunch, imagining that a hundred years ago, the children of Boreraig did the same. Of course, the truth might be more nuanced. In the 1860s Alexander Smith, on his travels around the island, saw 'two bare-footed and bare-headed girls yoked to a harrow and dragging it up and down a small plot of delved ground'. He describes the typical 'Skye hut', several of which he had visited, as 'smoky, dimly lit, open to the wind, pervious to the rain, floor of beaten earth, and with scanty furniture'. He contrasts these scenes on Skye to the squalor of the worst parts of Edinburgh in his day that he compares with scenes from Dante's Inferno where 'men have faces which hurt more than a blow would: of infants poisoned with gin, of children bred for the prisons and the hulks', and concludes, 'in one of these smoky cabins I would a thousand-fold rather spend my days than in Cowgate in Edinburgh or in one of the streets that radiate from Seven Dials'.

*

In the centre of the lawn, a tall man with flowing blond hair and stubble reminiscent of Bob Geldof was packing his tent. He asked me where I'd walked from, so I told him about my journey.

He replied: 'I started at Rubha Hunish on Monday and walked the whole Trotternish ridge in clouds and rain before the weather improved two days ago. So, I've delayed my departure this morning to make the most of Skye before finishing at Broadford this evening.'

Waterfall at Boreraig

'Well, you couldn't have found a more perfect place to camp,' I said, looking around, before enquiring about the route ahead. 'Is there any sort of a path between here and Torrin?'

'It's more or less a Land Rover track for the next few miles before the path narrows to climb around the cliff before broadening out again up the side of Loch Slapin.' I only just managed to restrain myself from hugging him at this news, and my ankles shouted in joy. Andy, as was his name, also told me that there was a burger van at Torrin, which was more good news considering my dire food situation. I left him to pack up in peace before going to find water and calculated that on a good path, I could probably make the six miles to Torrin by lunchtime.

The path proved to be an absolute joy, as promised – like a mown strip of grass flanked by bracken – and I bounced along like a hare out of a trap, all the time with the sea on my left and ever-rising cliffs on my right. Soon, just as Andy had said, the path narrowed and skirted up and around the headland on a terrace traverse that reminded me of a coastal run I did in Sicily earlier that year at the Zingaro Nature Reserve, but the azure-blue Mediterranean was replaced by the hazy-blue Sound of Rùm. At the brow of the hill, I said a final farewell to Loch Eishort, who had been my capricious companion for the last two days. But I'll give the final word on Loch Eishort to Alexander Smith, for whom – like me – it left a lasting impression:

On a fine morning there is not in the whole world a prettier sheet of water than Loch Eishart [sic]. Every thing about it is wild, beautiful and lonely. You drink a strange and unfamiliar air. You seem to be sailing out of the nineteenth century away back into the ninth. You are delighted and there is no remembered delight with which you can compare the feeling. Over the Loch the Cuchullins [sic] rise crested with tumult of golden mists; the shores are green behind; and away out, towards the horizon, the Island of Rum – ten miles long at the least – shorts up from the sea like pointed flame.

And then, just a few steps further on, just around the bend, Loch Slapin appeared below, jutting north towards the interior of Skye: a welcome way-marker. The loch was flanked by hills, foremost of which were the Black Cuillins; it felt like weeks ago that I first glimpsed their distinctive profile from on the skyline above Armadale: backwards-facing nose; horse's saddle; chameleon's head, back and tail; volcano; dragon's wings... I shared this moment of wonder with a newly shaven sheep who claimed the viewpoint as her own.

The path held more delights as it curved around the shore of the loch, revealing the round-topped Red Cuillins to the right. In shape, they were reminiscent of

(Top): Sheep guarding the path
(Bottom): Suisnish and Loch Slapin

the rolling Cheviots in Northumberland but much more massive in scale, and if I squinted, the bare rocks on top blushed sun-kissed peach.

Halfway up the loch, I met a couple of walkers huddled together, eating under the shade of the only tree. They had European accents, possibly German, and gave me a cheery 'hi' as they boiled their stove. Like Andy, they were interested in meeting someone walking in the opposite direction and wondered if I was doing the Skye Trail in reverse. They overlooked a rocky bay lapped by water so clear it was almost transparent: Camas Malag.

Thinking this would be my last chance to cool off for several days, I dipped behind rocks, changed and swam out. I lay on my back, allowing water, hills and sky to envelop me. Rejuvenated, I motored towards Torrin for a late lunch.

*

Approaching the end of the bay, I encountered a single-track metalled road where a white BMW was parked on the verge. The car jarred like a shard of glass against the towering black gabbro Cuillins behind. Sheep and cows grazed nearby. As the sun beat down, two of the vehicle's inhabitants were down at the water's edge, bouncing up and down on a pump, struggling to inflate a kayak like a scene from a Laurel and Hardy film. A third person spectated, hands on hips, planted like an A-frame. It seemed too hot to bother.

I followed the road up a shallow incline until a large quarry appeared on my left. I'm used to seeing slate quarries in the Lake District, grey stone against grey hills, but this was a stark juxtaposition of piles of brilliant white limestone against the rose-tinted whale-back of the Red Cuillins. Later, I was amused to read on their website that 'through careful design and screening as well as progressive restoration, our sites blend in well to their natural surroundings'. Not that the incursion vexed me. I find the aesthetics of industrial landscapes as visually interesting as natural, just in a different way, although those Meccano lines are slowly vanishing in North East England: Blyth Aluminium Smelter, Swan Hunter's Shipyard and Redcar Blast Furnace, that was brought down like one of the giant aliens in War of the Worlds. Tracy pulls my leg on country walks when she finds me loitering in the bushes inspecting an electricity substation for oil leaks, or peering over a fence into a factory looking for black smoke: 'You're not at work now!'.

The operations of this quarry were exposed for all to see from the road: site porta-cabins and weighbridge; grading machines with conveyor belts tilted like the necks of cranes; yellow excavators with gaping metal scoops signalled in the sunshine; a pair of vertical silos for storage; a rusty metal lockup, with a similar patina to the *Angel of the North*. All these sat proudly amongst a mini-mountain panorama of crushed limestone like a ski resort in mid-winter: The Alps on Skye.

As I walked on, I recalled a job I once did for a clay quarry in Cornwall, where, deep in the bowels of an apocalyptic lunar landscape, my guide suggested I tried my hand operating one of the powerful water jets, called a 'monitor', that rips the clay from the cliff. I stood inside a protective yellow cabin and manipulated a joystick to move the monster water pistol: up, down, left, right. It was like a homemade weapon from *Mad Max*. A water jet exploded from the monitor and dissolved the cliff like butter. The milky slurry then flowed downhill for treatment. Destructive, yes, but the clay, or Kaolin, is used to make porcelain, paper, paint, fibreglass and toothpaste.

*

Hungry as I was, the road to Torrin seemed interminably long as it wiggled past a hamlet called Ashbank and then around the base of the Beinn Dearg Mhor (Big Red Mountain), but I perked up when I saw a sign: 'HOT FOOD VAN – 1 MILE' by a cattle grid. Before reaching the van, I saw a purple-painted wooden shed marked 'TEA ROOM' situated in a gravel car park, so I headed for that. After dragging a small round picnic table into the shade of the building, I propped my backpack up against the seat and went to look inside. There was a long glass counter full of cakes, behind which an urn of soup bubbled away. I scanned for a menu on the tables, but they were bare, except for several occupied by couples eating their sweet treats.

Quarry near Torrin

I caught the attention of a woman serving behind the counter: 'Do you have any savoury food?' I enquired.

'We only sell soup and cakes here. There is a burger van down the hill, but he's closed today due to a power cut.'

Somewhat dismayed, I replied, 'Oh, I've walked from the ferry at Armadale over the last few days, and my food's gone off due to the heat. I'd love a cake, but I need something more savoury first; otherwise, I'll get a headache.'

'The soup is tomato if you would like that,' came the reply.

'Thanks, but I don't think I could face the soup in this heat; perhaps I could just have a slice of bread?'

'Sorry, we only sell the bread with the soup.'

I was neither in the mood for, nor capable of, pursuing the conversation, so I thought I'd just buy a drink and cook my last dried meal outside. But, as I retreated from the counter, a voice piped up from behind: 'We have some spare food in our campervan you are welcome to.' I spun around as a wiry man wearing a baseball cap stood up from a table in the corner and looked my way. I expressed my gratitude and followed him into the car park. He slid open the door on a classic VW camper, painted a delightful duck-egg blue with gleaming chrome hubcaps and white-on-black reg plates. (To a naturalist, it was the campervan equivalent of a resplendent Azure-winged Magpie.) He rummaged inside, opened the fridge and pulled out two bananas, a few slices of ham, a chunk of hard cheese, two raw fruit bars, and a bag of nuts. Receiving the food, I said they would help me reach Portree and offered him some notes, which I had squashed rolled up in my zip pocket, but he waved them away, saying, 'You might need those later'. I carefully stashed the food on my table and returned to purchase a cold can of coke, which I was served, along with the offer of free bread and butter to accompany my lunch. It was as if my benefactor's kind-heartedness was infectious. Needless to say, I munched through the tastiest banana, ham and cheese sandwiches of my life.

As I ate, I laid my map sections on the table, fitted them together like a jigsaw, and considered the route ahead. 'Plan A' was always to follow Paterson's route to the letter, but as my departure neared, I toyed with taking a detour to visit Loch Coruisk, which I'd read about in Robert Macfarlane's *The Wild Places* a few years ago. Macfarlane describes a hidden valley of almost mythic proportions: 'I felt a strong sense of having crossed a portal, or stepped over a threshold... a place that keeps Wild Time'. In my imagination, one might cross the threshold in this deep U-shaped valley and stumble into a fantasy world like Wakanda in the *Black Panther*. A hidden realm. In *A Summer in Skye*, Smith also attributes an otherworldly quality to Coruisk; he describes the party sailing in between the mountains, 'silent as a boatful of souls being conveyed to some Norse hades'. For him, the loch was the opposite of bucolic, he felt like an intruder where 'The hills seem to possess some secret; to brood over some unutterable idea which I can never know'.

Lunch stop at Torrin

The diversion to reach it would require me to swing left at the head of Loch Slapin and either climb over or around the Munro, Blàbheinn, that I'd previously discussed with my father, to reach a bulge in the coastline that skirts around the steeply-sided Sgurr na Stri. I would then need to cross a river at Camasunary before tackling the famous 'Bad Step' – a cliff that drops directly into the sea. From there, I could explore the shores of Coruisk, which thrust deep into the Cuillin Hills. In *The Wild Places*, at the head of the loch, Macfarlane ascended directly up the wall of the valley in an unsuccessful attempt to climb the Inaccessible Pinnacle, whereas I would stay at ground level and contour around the far side of the loch before rejoining Paterson's route in Glen Sligachan. I'd handwritten mile markers for two options on my map: Torrin to Glen Sligachan was seven miles directly across the mountain pass, while Loch Coruisk was 18 miles; Portree was another 14 miles after that. I looked up from my map across Loch Slapin and the intimidating dragon-back ridge of Blàbheinn glared back. Knowing I only had one dried meal left, I resigned myself to Plan A. Loch Coruisk – *'that has no interest in conforming to any human schedules'* – would have to remain safely ensconced between the pages of a book, at least for now. But, one day, I hope to return to experience it with Tracy.

Before leaving the cafe, the proprietor refilled my water bottles and told me that each summer they get hundreds of people walking the Skye Trail, but only two or three doing the original route from Armadale, which, given the pathless terrain, deer fences and deep gorges, made sense. I also found a large, cured sausage in a fridge, which hadn't been mentioned earlier. So, resupplied and replete, I meticulously repacked my items, scouted the table, bench and gravel floor for anything left behind, and continued on my way.

The narrow tarmac road to the top end of Loch Slapin was by now a furnace, so I walked on the grass verge, which was marginally cooler. The water shimmered, and the surrounding hills baked like potatoes in an oven. I protected myself by reapplying suncream and was grateful for my cap, sunglasses and snood that I'd fashioned into a kind of Lawrence of Arabia headscarf to protect my ears and neck. Nevertheless, my spirits were high as I embarked on the second phase of my journey: 'The Mountains'.

*

Paterson writes, 'From Torrin follow the Elgol road around the head of Loch Slapin. Soon after crossing the bridge of the Abhainn an' t-Stratha Mhoir, strike out right across moorland towards the mouth of the corrie contained by the twin east ridges of Garbh-bheinn'. I crossed the bridge and headed for a deep valley that curved upwards, containing a lively cascading stream. 'A charming series of smooth white quartz baths connected by short glissades and miniature falls', as Paterson eloquently describes it. I've never visited the so-called fairy pools on Skye that are said to be overcrowded on sunny days, but here, you could have a dozen pools to yourself in perfect tranquillity. I didn't stop, however, because the sun had disappeared behind a vast black cliff on my left, and I was beginning to think about where to camp.

As I climbed, the valley became steeper, and I craned my neck to scan the rocky ridge above for the crossing point: 'Bealach na Bèiste'. Paterson makes out it's a relatively easy pull up to the col, but for me, it was a tricky scramble where one wrong hold would have sent me tumbling back down the mountain. Not far from the top, I found a small ledge, carefully removed my pack, squashed my back to the cliff and took a long drink of water. From there, I had an eagle's view: the valley below, now in deep shade; Torrin, a cluster of houses and trees; Loch Slapin, a streak of blue stretching towards Sleat on the horizon.

Finally, I pulled myself onto the col and was rewarded with a small triangle of exposed flat land buffeted by wind. It was just past six o'clock, so I thought I might make it around the back of Garbh-bheinn to lower ground in Glen Sligachan to camp. I'd remembered from Paterson's route description that I must find a line of derelict metal fence posts on the far side of the mountain that contoured around Garbh-bheinn before climbing up to a second col and dropping into the glen – about two miles. It's a circuitous route but avoids climbing up a steeper and higher pass at the head of the valley. After 15 minutes, I located the first of the rusty metal posts that stretched into the distance under a looming granite cliff. But, the ground was steep and stony, the light was rapidly fading, the way ahead uncertain. I was benighted.

The way ahead up Allt Aigeinn to Bealach na Bèiste

Turning around is never easy on a long walk, but I decided my least-worst option was to retrace my steps back up to the small patch of flat ground at Bealach na Bèiste. By the time I'd returned, the wind had strengthened, so with some trepidation, I pitched my ephemeral tent in the midst of this mighty mountain arena. It looked like pitiful protection from the elements, so I secured the guy ropes with heavy rocks. Then, I cooked my last dried meal on my stove, around which I fashioned an aluminium foil screen to stop it from blowing out. As I ate, the sun set to the west, the direction from which I'd retreated, and illuminated my tent like a lantern.

Despite the wind, my elevated location had three advantages over previous pitches: it was cooler; there were no midges – 'hooray!'; and for the first evening, I could get a phone signal so I could update Tracy on my progress. I also asked her to text me a photograph of Paterson's route description for tomorrow because although I had highlighted it on my paper map and saved it as a GPX track on my phone, I guessed correctly that I'd be in the clouds by morning.

I bunged up my ears with plugs and squashed deep into my sleeping bag but felt as exposed as an ant on the east face of Everest.

Calm before the storm at Bealach na Bèiste

6. TEMPEST IN SLIGACHAN

Day 4: Bealach na Bèiste to Portree, 19 miles

The wind shook my tent with increasing ferocity, a membrane between me and the storm. I counted the seconds between gusts, wondering if the next would rip my tent apart. Each blast funnelled up the mountain: an elongated 'Voooosh' before careering over the bealach and hitting with a bang. A Chinese dragon uncoiling up the hill, cresting the ridge in a fury. The Dyneema fabric rustled violently as raindrops mazed down the fly sheet, while my upturned trekking poles provided the only structural support. The handles sank deeper into the softening ground, and the metal tips strained against the shallow eyelets woven into the apex. I wished those eyelets had been made a fraction deeper. I repeatedly checked the poles for slippage and quickly opened the flick locks to extend them, pushing them a hair's width further apart while holding my breath. Beneath me, bubbles stared upwards under the groundsheet like globules of trapped frogspawn or disembodied eyes. The transparent groundsheet – that weighs less than a feather but is said to be stronger than steel – held the wetness at bay, but not the cold, as my shelter doubled up as a raft. It was simultaneously thrilling and terrifying. The constructs of civilisation peeled away. The edges of my existence became permeable.

In his *Ecclesiastical History of the English People,* Bede described how life is fleeting, like a sparrow flying swiftly through a feasting hall in wintertime: out of the darkness, wind and rain and then, for the briefest of moments, into the warmth and calm where the wintery tempest cannot touch it. 'So, this life of man appears for a moment; what follows or indeed what went before, we know not at all.' I felt the void outside the hall that night: rock, water, wind.

Eventually, the darkness receded, replaced by a grey diffuse light. I dressed in the tent, wrapped myself in all my layers, and securely closed the zips before emerging into the maelstrom. Wind tore at the mountain, dragging clouds behind it, eager to spill over the ridge and drown the land. I still wore my earplugs yet struggled to hear myself think. It took me all my strength to pack up my tent without it ripping away. Foolishly, I removed most of the pegs before lowering the poles, and the tent, shackled all night, finally broke free, metamorphosising into a vampire jellyfish. One of the pole tips scraped across the fabric before I wrestled the whole mess to the ground.

Dyneema is supposed to be 'rolled, not stuffed', but I unceremoniously stuffed it into the sack, still wet. Before leaving the beastly bealach, I returned most of the rocks I'd used to secure the pegs to their original positions and checked the area for anything left behind.

I walked on a compass bearing, due west, to relocate the metal fence, now partially veiled by clouds and scoured by wind. I re-read Paterson's directions on my phone, zooming into the image Tracy sent me: Follow the semi-broken fence until it turns uphill. Cross a lively burn. Contour below steep black cliffs before cutting leftward up a 'broad, easy, grassy gully' through the rocky slopes at a ridge. Turn left and climb to Point 489, which has uninterrupted 360-degree views.

I progressed uneasily around the mountain as water coursed off the cliff. Then, the clouds parted in the valley below to reveal a flash of bounding white rumps of a skirr of deer. The valley was wide, steep and remote, but the herd traversed it in minutes, flowing down one side before fording the river and dissolving into the grass and heather on the other – no human vehicle could have crossed more swiftly and with apparently such little effort. They were the only deer I saw that week on Skye.

I scrambled up the so-called 'broad, easy grass gully' on all fours to reach an exposed ridge before heading uphill to Point 489 in thick cloud. There wasn't much to see on the summit, just a wet, rusty fence post protruding from a pile of lichen-encrusted rocks. Nevertheless, I paused to take a photo of myself, crouching down so I wasn't blown off my feet.

Getting wet at Point 489

I was now roughly halfway across Skye, and had the visibility been good, I might have had views north up Glen Sligachan towards Portree and perhaps even the Trotternish Ridge beyond. Paterson describes a panoramic view encompassing the bold profile of the Red Hills to the east, with the island of Scalpay and Raasay beyond; Garbh-bheinn and the twin-headed Bla Bheinn to the south; the serrated ridge of the Cuillin to the west; and the steep south ridge of Marsco to the north. Marsco caught my attention as a potential mountain to climb when planning the walk, as it lies almost on the route between where I was crouching and Sligachan. The Walk Highlands website describes it as the finest of the Red Hills, but I could only think about getting off the mountain as quickly as possible, so I followed another ruined fence line west, down and down into the Glen. Raindrops needled my face, and I battled against a torrent of wind as if I were in an Aeolian wrestling competition. But as I lost altitude, I picked up speed and bounded over the soft, spongy ground, imitating the red deer I'd seen earlier, assisted by the lack of weight on my back.

I rounded the skirt of Marsco and landed on the broad path that ferries hikers up Glen Sligachan from the Sligachan Hotel. I lashed my poles to my pack and fished out the cured sausage I'd purchased in Torrin, the last of my provisions. I munched and walked. Water streamed off every surface: my hood, the sausage, the path. Rainbows, stacked two high, leapt across the Glen, forming and unforming like technicolour slinky springs. I'd never seen so many in one place.

Rainbows in Glen Sligachan

I had the mighty Sligachan to myself except for a couple of brave souls venturing up from the hotel: he had earthy features and was wearing regular hiking gear while she sported a clear plastic bag with armholes thrown over a leotard. The plastic was embossed with dozens of gold stars, giving the whole ensemble the appearance of a sprite. Picture the scene – water, rainbows, a vision of elementals – we were even on an island: *The Tempest*. I asked myself if Prospero's cave was around the corner. Indeed, Alexander Smith made a similar comparison in *A Summer in Skye* commenting on the prevalence of Second Sight amongst the locals: 'There has been something weird and uncanny about the island for some centuries; it is haunted by legends; as full of noises as Prospero's Island.'

We shared a snatch of conversation, as people do when confronting a common adversary: 'Lovely weather! Glorious rainbows!' and, somewhat uninhibited from my days of vagabonding in the wilderness, complimented her on her sprite-like appearance, 'I love your outfit, with all its stars; you could be the faerie of the Glen', to which I received a cheerful laugh, quite at odds with the lashing rain. I asked them where they were headed – 'We're hoping to reach Loch Coruisk' came the optimistic reply from the man. I wished them luck but filed the information on their whereabouts.

Conveniently, I arrived at the whitewashed Sligachan Hotel around lunchtime, and as I had nothing else to eat, considered going inside. But first, I stood on a stone bridge, obstacled with warm tourists emerged from idling cars. Like them, I marvelled at the view up the valley – a grand master of brooding clouds and blinds of rain, veiling and unveiling the moody angular face of Masco, whose name means Seagull in Norse and is infamous for appearing on the album cover of *Organisation* by Orchestral Manoeuvres in the Dark; Sgurr nan Gillean rose into the cloud on the other side of the valley, the mountain I climbed with Mark 25 years ago; an angry torrent of water said to have rejuvenating properties, gushed under the bridge. A windswept wonderland.

Cameras snapped, tee shirts flapped, blouses gaped, and hair came undone. Black boots, white trainers, pink pumps, sparkly sandals. A brave few ventured as far as a statue of two chiselled mountain climbers, one standing and one sitting on top of a pile of boulders, gazing horizonward: John Mackenzie and Norman Collie. I was shocked to suddenly be surrounded by so many people and simultaneously felt pleasure and agoraphobia.

Sligachan was already a famous halting-place for tourists in Alexander Smith's day, and he stopped here for lunch, 'dining on trout which a couple of hours before were darting hither and thither in the steam'. His description of the surrounding hills was less favourable: 'Monstrous, abnormal, chaotic, they resemble the other hills on the earth's surface as Hindoo deities resemble human beings'.

I entered the vast, hall-like restaurant and was hit by a cacophony of sensations: heat, noise, moving pictures on TV screens, and immediately felt dislocated – like Bede's sparrow. Nevertheless, I needed to eat, so asked the waitress if they accepted hikers, which they did. She kindly

Looking up Glen Sligachan from Sligachan Bridge

showed me to a table in the far corner, with lots of space around it, so I could dry out my tent a little while I ate. I felt like I was suffocating, so opened the window behind me to let in some fresh air. I also used a power socket to charge my phone and battery pack and a toilet to change. I checked the route to Portree as I ate: three miles along the edge of Loch Sligachan to the east coast and nine miles north along minor roads. Despite my slow progress so far, I guessed I could cover the distance in about five hours. At the end of my meal, I folded up my tent and methodically stowed everything back in my pack.

*

Under pressure to reach Portree by nightfall, the afternoon's walk had the feel of an endurance challenge, and I clocked sights as I marched: a posse of male hikers passing me on the loch path with rucksacks covered in an array of primary colours, juxtaposed against the grey sky; a seal, which at first I thought was a porpoise, surfing on a wave; a small ferry plying its trade from Sconser to Raasay; a red phone box converted into a miniature library and defibrillator shelter; a cairn marking the 'Battle of the Braes' in 1882; a tiny black rabbit sat in the road; a sapling sprouting from the top of a fence post; a pretty, sweet smelling flower in a hedgerow, composed of clusters of tiny pink and white lantern-like florets, which I photographed and messaged to Tracy.

Library phone box at Peinchorran

In *A Long Walk*, Paterson explains that the cairn was the site of the last battle fought on British soil when 60 local crofters fought the police, who were brought in to enforce summary evictions. The protesters were arrested, convicted and fined, and, in contrast to the tranquil seas I'd swam in on Sleat, 'warships were despatched to patrol the island's water and troops landed to cow the people into submission'. Colonisation. Possession. Dispossession.

*

I arrived in Portree at 7pm, exhausted. I searched for accommodation on my phone and discovered an official campsite about two miles north, but I wasn't sure if they would take latecomers, and I didn't fancy arriving in the dark. I passed a long row of neat houses with bed and breakfast signs on the drive, all slid to 'NO VACANCIES'. I searched on my phone for accommodation, but again, everything was full. Somewhat at a loss of what to do, I hobbled down to the harbour, where a large public car park looked over a thin strip of mown grass with picnic tables and a salt marsh beyond. Already pitched on the grass were two tents, which seemed like an insalubrious place to camp. Up from the car park was a cheery blue 'Hostelling Scotland' sign affixed to a red brick building with lights blazing from the common room. My feet automatically led me past the wheely bins and up the steps to the front door, to which there was a sign blu-tacked to the inside stating that the hotel was full. *Perhaps I could sleep on the floor?* Through the door, I hovered nervously at the desk and waited to get the receptionist's attention. 'Hello!' I said cheerily. 'I saw the sign outside, but I'm doing the Skye Trail and just wondered if you had any room tonight?'

The young lad glanced at his book, looked up, and threw me a half smile. 'Yes, we've just had a cancellation and have one bed left in a male dorm. £29 for the night.'

'I'll take it!' I paid for the room and hired a fluffy white towel before installing myself in my bunk. I was greeted by a lean, ancient, reaper-like man with an American accent and a rakish one-syllable name I've forgotten, but it was something like Chuck, Lex or Zac. He was on a world tour with his wife, who must have been in the next dorm, and gave me a brief account of his travels through Scandinavia before bedding down at around 8pm. We were on the lower of two opposing bunks; the dorm had six other beds, as yet unoccupied.

I've stayed in hostels several times, but I prefer the isolation of my tent. It's not that I dislike people, I just prefer them spread out. I always worry about dorm etiquette: switching on the light, sharing the only peg, going to the toilet, setting off the fan, snoring. But I figured I was pretty well prepared for a night at the hostel, kitted out with a head torch, Kindle with a back-lit screen and ear plugs. However, I did apologise to my American friend that I'd probably have to get up at night to use the facilities. He said that he would too.

I took a rejuvenating shower before negotiating the tiny local co-op, with aisles about one-and-a-half persons wide, to buy bread and eggs for dinner and cereal and milk for breakfast. Back at the hostel, I summoned the last of my energy to poach a couple of eggs in the shiny steel kitchen before savouring the fresh food in the dining room where small groups sat around on chairs and benches chatting. It wasn't long before I crept into the dorm.

7. A FRIEND IN PORTREE

Day 5: Portree to south of Storr, 7 miles

It was after lunch before I set off through dreich Portree and made my way to the harbour where the famous row of multi-coloured shops did their best to cheer up the day, their muted hues tessellating in the water below. A blanket of clouds shrugged over the low hills behind the town, lending a myopic vibe, bringing to mind the detective series *Shetland*. I imagined the comings and goings of the fishing boats tethered side-by-side to the industrial pier, their fishing gear raised like wary crabs.

Before leaving Portree, I had an appointment with The Cuillin Hills Hotel, an establishment at the opposite end of the price spectrum from the hostel I'd just vacated, and a short walk from the harbour. At the bottom of the hotel drive, I examined an information sign that gave details of the local wildlife and a short circular walk around a headland called Scorrybreac. As I read, I was approached by a well-heeled American couple waving a

Portree

grainy paper map. 'Hiya, are you doing the trail? We've been given this map by the hotel but can't make head or tail of it.' I studied the map briefly and saw their route matched the description on the sign. 'Yes,' I replied, pointing along a track, 'I think if you follow the coastline along this path, you will be on the right path.' Just before I headed off, a tall, younger man appeared wearing a large red backpack, an orange waterproof jacket, and a large camera slung around his neck. When he heard the couple talking, he asked them where they were from. 'North Dakota' came the reply. 'Me too,' he said, 'but I now live in Amsterdam.' The air fizzed as the threesome made connections and talked longingly about their sparsely populated home state, swapping notes about places and memories. People often do this when abroad, becoming instant friends with folks with whom they probably would pass by in their hometown. I guess we all long for connection with our tribe, and the further we are away from home, the stronger that connection grows. If I hear a Geordie accent abroad, my ears spin like a cat.

I wound up the long, wooded drive to the hotel, passing expensive Land Rovers, Audis and MGs, grateful for the shower last night, which I hoped had rendered my appearance and odour slightly less offensive. I passed a glass-fronted dining room with a view of the iconic harbour, where well-dressed residents were picking clean morsels of shellfish, possibly harvested on Loch Eishort. Shells were piled up, they'd eaten every one.

As inconspicuously as possible, I entered the grand double doors, wiped my feet on the mat, and trundled across to the large reception desk. 'Oh, hello, my name's Marek Bidwell,' I said to the lady behind the desk, putting on my best voice, 'I'm walking the Skye Trail. I called the hotel a few weeks ago to ask if I could send a parcel to collect on my way past and wondered if you have received it?'

The receptionist gave me a warm smile, reached under the desk, and pulled out the large brown padded envelope I last saw two weeks ago that had seemingly travelled in space and time. I noticed it was opened, and my note had been removed and presumably read. 'Yes, here it is,' she replied, 'we've been expecting you.'

Relieved my plan had worked, I thanked her, and I told her a bit about my walk: 'The weather was superb until I reached the mountains and then a storm hit–'

'Oh, yes, my son climbed Sgùrr Alasdair, the highest of the Cuillins, a few days ago in the good weather with friends. He said they could see the whole island from the top!' We chatted convivially, but not wanting to outstay my welcome and get mixed up with the hotel guests, after a few minutes, I scooped up my parcel, cradling it like a baby, and retreated outside, casting a glace through the dining room window.

I found a quiet spot back down the hill by the shore with a picnic bench and meticulously checked off every item before stowing them in my pack. So that was it: hoist pack, tightened straps, deep breath, onward bound.

*

With new resolve, I strode northwards along a slender track that hugged the coast. Before me loomed the renowned Trotternish ridge, which is said to be one of the finest walks in Britain. I recalled images of this land that adorns my study at home, postcards that my parents and friends had mailed me over the years: rock needles rising above cloud inversions like geological totem poles. The images pulled me northwards. The way ahead was divided into three parts: eight miles crossing the escarpment north of Portree, the highest point of which is named Sìthean a' Bhealaich Chumhaing on the map, poetically translates as 'Narrow Pass of the Faries'; then, 14 miles along the Beinn Edra ridge, the start of which is guarded by the Old Man of Storr that stands sentinel; and finally, eight miles across the last finger of high ground where the earth had spilt and cracked into a mosaic of tabled landslips known as the Quiraing, before descending to journey's end at Rubna Hunish.

As I approached the first climb of the afternoon, up to Creag Mhòr (Big Crag), a colony of honking ravens swirled around the cliff top in a great uproar. Then, a much larger bird soared away from the rooks toward me, just below the cliff's rim. It had long, broad wings that it occasionally flapped to gain altitude and mewed like a buzzard. I tracked it with my binoculars until it settled on the corner of another crag like a bookend silhouetted against the sky. I snapped a grainy photo of it on my phone, and looking at it now, enlarged on my computer, I want to believe I can make out the yellow bill of a White-Tailed Eagle. I'll let you be the judge.

Grainy phone photo of a White-Tailed Eagle?

As I approached the foot of the hill, I saw the man in the orange jacket I'd met earlier talking to the American couple. He was studying a map and asked me which way I thought the route went up the hill. Between us, we picked out a sketchy path up a gully, where we stopped to fill our water bottles before reaching the ridge. As we walked, he told me, with a confident twang, that he was 'Logan from South Dakota' and was walking The Skye Trail from South to North – 'Why end in a pub in Broadford when you can finish on a cliff top overlooking the Outer Hebrides?' – a sentiment I shared. We talked about kit: he wore leather boots that had sprung a leak, carried a two-person tent, and wore a tiny device on his shoulder strap. 'It's a Garmin GPS that allows my wife, back in Amsterdam, to track my movements. It's not cheap, and you must subscribe, but you only pay for the months you need.' I thought back to my worries about being unable to contact Tracy whilst on Sleat and considered investing in one for my next trip. Then, the conversation meandered between life in North Dakota, Amsterdam, and Newcastle: culture, food, housekeeping.

On reaching the top of the hill, with the escarpment tumbling down to the sea to our right, like a tiered wedding cake, we took photos of each other with the Isle of Raasay in the background. I had a hiking buddy for the first time on this trip, and the next few miles passed quickly. A pleasant walk, a pleasant talk, above the briny beach.

Just as I was thinking about where to camp for the night and wondered if we might share a spot, Logan suddenly exclaimed, 'Oh, I've dropped my camera hood. I can't go on without it!' We looked around together on the hillside, but eventually, he decided to retrace his steps. I wished him luck and continued alone.

By the time I passed the trig point at the 'Narrow Pass of the Fairies', I was in thick cloud and not a fairy was to be seen. Strong gusts buffeted me from the side, so I pushed on for a couple of miles to a more sheltered spot. I pitched my tent in the gloom and settled down with my book for the night.

Hiking companion

8. THE BIG OLD MAN

Day 6: South of Storr to Bealach Uige, 14 miles

It rained heavily during the night, but by the time I was ready to set off, the clouds had started to disperse, giving good views north over a loch towards The Storr, but the Old Man himself was still hidden beneath a giant fluffy caterpillar of cloud crawling out to sea. As I studied the terrain, I noticed another tent about four hundred yards ahead; I wondered if it was Logan, but there was no sign of his bright orange jacket.

I packed up and headed across boggy rain-drenched grass towards the loch. There, gazing across the water, I got my first glimpse of the rock pinnacles on the far hillside needling the underside of the cloud. Then, a rainbow arched across the loch from shore to shore just as the cloud lowered and a squall hit me from the west. I pulled my waterproofs tighter and crossed the loch on a bridge that formed a dam. Emanating from the dam wall, two large pipes snaked a mile or so to the coast, where I guessed there was a hydroelectric power station.

Looking north from campsite towards Old Man of Storr

The pipes reminded me of a walk in a different world many years ago with my sister when she lived in Nigeria. We'd ventured out from the bustle of Jos to the edge of the plateau to follow the 'aqueduct trail'. We walked through a landscape of thorny scrub from a reservoir along the route of an aqueduct – sometimes open like a flume where groups of people gathered to wash their clothes and in other places enclosed in a pipe – that flowed to the edge of the cliff, where it dropped almost vertically hundreds of feet to a power plant. We ate my sister's peanut butter and egg rolls for lunch on a large concrete foundation at the edge of the plateau overlooking a parched hillside of leafless trees bristling with extravagant red flowers.

Back on Skye, the hillside ahead was anything but parched, and when I reached a road, I sheltered in a bus stop, hoping the rain would pass. It didn't. The car park was nothing more than a long layby in which there must have been between 50 to 60 vehicles, many still inhabited with families sheltering. A few hardy souls, some in shorts, tortoised to the pay station, necks withdrawn into jackets. As I walked past the steamed-up vehicles – all kitted up with my tent on my back – I felt sorry for those inside: the thought of rain is worse than the rain itself, the transition from one state to another.

While writing this book, I've been reading *About Grace* by Anthony Doerr, one of my favourite writers who animates *place* as well as *people*. The protagonist, Winkler, a hydrologist, spends his life's savings trying to find his daughter after his estranged partner, Sandy, dies. Eventually, he tracks her down to discover he now has a grandson whom he takes to plant a tree on Sandy's grave. It's raining, and Christopher doesn't want to get out of the car:

> "Rain is always worse hearing it on the roof. But once you're out in it, moving around, it'll feel kind of good. You'll see." The boy's eyes turned up, as if calculating whether or not the rain would feel good.

About Grace is all about transitions. Snow falling and snow melting. Water evaporating and water condensing. Insects hibernating and insects cocooning. Convergence and divergence. Seasons. Winkler fleeing from frozen Alaska to exile in the sun-bleached Caribbean where he languishes for 25 years before re-emerging.

*

I climbed a winding path that I supposed was getting closer to the Old Man, but the swirling mist gave little away. I read several sturdy information boards about the landscape, the text obscured by raindrops. They told me that the escarpment above is composed of heavy volcanic rock sitting on softer sedimentary rock, the cause of the many landslips. The volcanic rock was formed around 60 million years ago from lava flows erupting from fissures; the whole area has been repeatedly covered in ice, and the landscape is still changing, with a large rockfall in the summer of 2004. The Old Man of Storr broke free from the escarpment around 6100 years ago, which is after the last ice age, so it is still sharp and spiky.

I also learned some more words, not in Gaelic, but in Norse, giving a clue to the island's history: An Stòr means 'big', and the pinnacle is named 'Bodach an Stòir', which must literally translate as 'Big Old Man'. The whole landscape has been classified as an outdoor museum called 'Druim nan Linntean' or 'Ridge of Ages', which, I think, is back to Gaelic.

There was also a poem, written out in both Gaelic and English: a lament of the Highland Clearances and ode to the landscape, by Mary MacPearson (*Màiri Mhòr nan Oran*):

> *Farewell to the place*
> *Where I spent my youth,*
> *Island of the high mountains*
> *Where the mist rests;*
> *On which rises early*
> *The rose-coloured sun in the sky,*
> *Chasing away the clouds of night,*
> *Illuminating the Storr.*

More transitions.

By now, I was being pelted by the rain, and the drops were bouncing off my jacket like hail. Ironically, I was thirsty, having used all my water from last night and failing to find a suitable stream. I'd considered a few small rivulets running off the path, but they were all full of eroding sediment. Ahead of me, lances of driving rain swept like skimmed stones over a small tarn. And just when the rain was strongest, a woman, 'June from California', stopped to talk to me. She asked where I was staying and was amazed that I was wild camping and had been walking north for five days to reach this spot. In turn, I asked if she knew about the Pacific Crest Trail that runs through California. She wished me luck.

Miraculously, as I plodded around the next few bends, the weather gods relented and the Old Man and his companions loomed above me, standing sentinel on the horizon: stricken ramparts guarding a giant's cauldron of boiling vapours. Walking amongst these monumental formations, I felt humbled: rocky fingers pointing skywards as if in accusation or connection. Earth and sky. Gaia and Uranus. Geology and mythology.

After admiring, even venerating, these natural monuments, I found it difficult to tear myself away, and I set my heart on returning one day. Before the path threaded behind the mountain, I stopped on a promontory and looked back along with about twenty other people, all vying for the perfect photo. One girl stood with her hands held aloft in a 'V' shape for the perfect Instagram image. She looked genuinely inspired.

My onward path crossed a small stile and then did a dog-leg contouring around the mountain's north side. The transformation was total: crowds to isolation, hubbub to silence. I stopped by a fast-flowing stream to fill my water bottles, guessing that the precious two litres would have to last me for the next 12 miles.

Old Man of Storr above Loch Leathan

Old Man of Storr

Ahead, the highest section of the Trotternish escarpment unfurled like a vertical ribbon of rock wafting backwards and forwards to the horizon. The walking on sheep-nibbled grass was easy, freeing me to admire the light playing on the undulating shelves of land below, cascading into the sea. Occasionally, an exceptionally breathtaking scene gave me pause. An untamed river meandering from the foothills to the coast – a lesson in hydrology and perspective. A close-up view of the escarpment's edge: dark columnar rocks reminiscent of Northumberland's Whin Sill on which stand Hadrian's Wall and Bamburgh Castle. Moon-white rock of the Isle of Rona swimming in the sea between Skye and the mainland, framed by basalt.

It was perfect walking weather; the rain had cleared and it was cooler than before. I savoured each moment, gathering them up like stones: *lucky I am to be here now, putting one foot in front of another, traversing the top of the world*. Great airships of white cloud drifted west, skimming the top of the escarpment before suddenly finding themselves a thousand feet up and continuing their journey, imperious, gracing the coastal plain with mackerel shadow pictures, or *rionnach maoim* according to Robert Macfarlane's wordhoard in *Landmarks*. And as my legs ate the distance, the sun arced west, and the escarpment cast elongated tentacles over the plain; by six-thirty, they touched the sea.

Once past the summit trig point of Beinn Edra, I scouted for somewhere to camp. The only patches of short grass were perilously close to the cliff, while further

Summit of Beinn Edra

inland, the vegetation soon turned into a soggy bog. I pitched my tent just off the path but couldn't settle. A stiff wind blew directly toward the cliff, and I had visions of sleepwalking over the edge. So, with consternation, I decamped and continued northwards down the ridge. It turned out to be a good decision because, after about 20 minutes, I found the perfect spot at a shallow col called Bealach Uige. On the landward side of the path was a circle of stones around a flat lawn of grass. As the sun illuminated the western horizon with a golden glow – the final act of a dazzling day's opera – I pitched my tent for the second time inside the welcoming stone circle. Then, as usual, I screwed my burner to the gas bottle and struck a match. *Squish*. The pink tip turned to mush on the damp box. I tried a second match. The same. A third, a fourth, a fifth: *squish, squish, squish*. I paused and counted my remaining matches. Seven. I berated myself for allowing them to get wet in a non-waterproof bag. I've never smoked cigarettes, so have little experience with matches, except for occasionally lighting the fire at home. If I couldn't light the stove, there would be no dinner. With just a slither of phone reception, I searched the internet one byte at a time for tips to light wet matches. It was slow going, but eventually, one website loaded with a list of suggestions: insert the match into the lamp end of a torch and hold up to the sun using the lens as a prism; rub the wet matches in your hair; strike match on a long length of dry wood; put the matches in the oven. Suggestions one and four were clearly out of the question because the sun had set and I'd carelessly left my oven at home. So, I tried number two: I rubbed four matches in my hair until a sheep sidled over and looked at me quizzically, and then attempted to get a spark. *Squelch.* Same result: the phosphorus tips disintegrated one by one. With just three matches left and a growing sense of futility, I tried to light them on the rocks that formed the stone circle, as there was no wood. I discerned a tiny glimmer of friction, like the tremor of a butterfly on landing, as one match scraped on the rock. Dinner? But the end rubbed off before it produced a flame. Three. Two. One. Gone.

Prometheus stole fire from the Gods and gave it to men... but not to Marek!

I considered my options. After resupplying in Portree, I still had a few wraps and some cheese, but I also wondered if it was safe to eat my freeze-dried meal cold. The writing on the back of the packet was tiny, and I strained my eyes to read it even with the aid of my headtorch. 'Usage Instructions: Store in a cool, dry place. Preparation Instructions: Remove oxygen absorber, add 350ml boiling water, stir for 8 minutes, Serve.' There was nothing about eating cold. If it hadn't been for my previous food poisoning incident in the North Pennines where, after a night of sickness, Tracy came to rescue me, I might have risked it; but it seemed foolhardy here, a long way from home, where I had only the sheep and incorporeal fairies for company. I never fully resolved the cause of that night's sickness: it could have been the food itself; the water I used to cook with, possibly contaminated by old lead mines; or my belief that the

Sunrise of day seven

silica gel sachet contained salt, like those in crisp packets I ate as a child. To this day, family members save their silica gel packets and pile them up on my mat at dinner!

So, I resigned myself to a second meal of the day of cold wraps and cheese. Despite feeling hungry, I struggled to chew and swallow as the temperature dropped. I know many backpackers only eat cold meals to save weight, but a hot meal is a birdhouse in my soul at the end of a long day. One concession to comfort. Nevertheless, it seemed churlish to be too upset after such a legendary day on the hills.

9. AMAZING SKYE

Day 7: Bealach Uige to Rubha Hunish, 11 miles

The day dawned bright and clear, and I watched the sun rise above a layer of sea-hugging cloud whilst I ate breakfast. To the north, the sun's rays lapped the edge of the escarpment, brushing a hundred hillocks in hues of amber and bronze with such finesse that they appeared to flow like liquified earth towards the sea. One landslip, more massive than the rest, rose from the plains like the plated back of a sleeping Stegosaurus. If I could have found a way down the cliff, exploring this mini mountain would have made for an exciting diversion. Aligning my map to the landscape, I saw that the elongated ring of contours was named Cleat. A thin blue line, the River Brogaig, ran down from Cleat to Staffin Bay, connecting my imaginary dinosaur to actual dinosaurs that once walked on Skye. There, on the coast in 2001, two dog walkers discovered a large triangular impression in a rock. Palaeontologists – or more precisely, ichnologists who study these highly transitory tracks – visited the

Looking north along the Trotternish Ridge to Cleat

site and found 18 other impressions that turned out to be dinosaur footprints made around 166 million years ago when the land that is now Skye was south of the equator and was a humid, muddy lagoon. Reptilian-shaped Cleat, however, is made of much more recent igneous rock, so no bard can claim Cleat to be the petrified maker of those prehistoric prints.

Skye beckoned me on as if it had deliberately withheld the best of its secrets to the last, and I continued to walk north along *Druim nan Linntean,* the Ridge of Ages. I followed the escarpment's edge around a sweeping curve between Beinn Edra and the next summit, Bioda Buidhe. On a lobe of land extending beyond the shelf overlooking Cleat, I passed two men packing up an enormous tunnel tent with at least a dozen guy ropes; they must have had a sublime view at sunrise from their vertiginous vantage point. They were busy with the guy ropes at 9am when I first saw them, and when I turned back to admire the view half an hour later from near the top of Bioda Buidhe, and their tent had shrunk to a dot in the landscape, they were still folding the fly sheet. From where I stood, the Trotternish Ridge resembled a giant cresting green wave chasing foaming landslips towards the sea.

Beyond the summit of Bioda Buidhe, the view north opened up again: a steep u-shaped gully funnelled the eye a thousand feet down to a hollow where tiny sapphire-blue lochs nestled amongst grassy emerald slopes. Beyond, the land rose to a pincushion of needle-like rocks spiking the skyline of the final high plateau on Skye: The Quiraing, or *Cuith-raing.*

It has long been a magnet for travellers, and Alexander Smith wrote, 'The Quiraing is one of the wonderful sights of Skye and if you once visit it you will believe ever afterwards the misty and spectral Ossian to be authentic.' (Ossian being a fabled blind bard, son of Fionn mac Cumhaill who built the Giant's Causeway.) 'The Quiraing is a nightmare of nature; 'tis a huge spire or cathedral of rock some thousand feet in height, with rocky spires or needles sticking out of it'.

With one eye always on the spectacle ahead, I descended a heathery slope and reached another car park, like the one I passed at The Storr, but today, the cars gleamed in the sunshine. People swanned about getting tickets from the machine and burgers from a van, admiring the view, outstretched like cormorants drying on a rock. Clothes were shed, spirits unfurled, gazes cast.

With so many people, it crossed my mind that one of them might have a spare match or cigarette lighter, so I asked around. After a few polite 'sorry, we're not smokers', a man who had already declined my request once called me back to his car brandishing a lighter: 'Here, you can take this; I'll pick up another from a shop on the way back.' The man wore a bulky leather biker's jacket and told me he was visiting from Germany before flicking the lighter a couple of times, demonstrating its efficacy. I thanked him profusely and explained how his gift would allow me to have a hot meal that evening. 'May you be eternally blessed,' I said benevolently in parting.

People at the Quiraing car park

After the car park, I had a critical route choice to make. Paterson's *A Long Walk* ascends the last section of the ridge above the tumbled rocks of the Quiraing, while The Skye Trail winds between them before veering east to the coastal village of Flodigarry. After the ease of walking on an actual path for the last few days, albeit faint in places, I had little desire to return to the tribulations of Sleat. So, whilst purchasing an inferior coffee from the snack van, I asked the vendor if he knew if there was a path over the hills to the north. 'I haven't walked the whole way, but I've seen people coming down Glen Scamadal on far other side; there's a deep scar on the northern flank, where a river runs north to near Duntulm.' So, with a belly full of watery coffee, I climbed the steep and eroded path up to the escarpment overlooking the Quiraing. People were ahead of me, people behind me, and even a drone buzzing above. Halfway up, I ventured as close to the edge as my nerves would allow and peered down at The Prison and The Needle, which rose up like the scales on a dragon's back, behind which was the crofting village Digg where each house was set in a neat rectangular strip of land like a green spreadsheet. Beyond Digg gentle waves broke onto crescent-shaped Staffin beach that circled around to Staffin Island. It was easy to imagine giants or dinosaurs inhabiting this majestic place. Such landscapes are a catalyst for creativity. Ossian's muse.

I passed the grassy summit of Meall na Suiramch, topped with a cairn, before contouring around the east flank of the hill. On my right, a solid stone path led onwards towards two enormous slabs of land that tilted up towards the coast like launch pads on an aircraft carrier. The map names one of these features 'Leac nan Fionn', or Fingal's tomb, that is the fabled resting place of the legendary warrior who is the subject of the *Poems of Ossian*, so loved by Alexander Smith. I started off down the path as a steady stream of people trudged up on a circular walk around the Quiraing, but soon I realised I'd been deceived by the view, and my route lay higher up, on the ridge.

*

The hoped for path gradually faded like mist on a summer's morning until I was back to a mile of bog hopping to the final summit at Sgùrr Mòr. There, I was rewarded with a view of the northern tip of the peninsula to rival all others: 'The Restaurant at the End of the Universe', the crow's nest on the HMS Beagle, the throne-room of Minas Tirith. A river meandered from the bottom of the cliff through a mosaic of wetland towards a deep inlet cut into the northeast coast, while due north, a finger of land pointed across a clear blue sea, towards a long strip of mountains on the horizon, mirrored by a slither of white clouds above. It could have been the land of the gods: Annwn, The Otherworld, or even Asgard. But my map assured me it was the Outer Hebrides. The adventure never ends!

Overlooking the Quiraing and Staffin Bay

Cairn on Sgùrr Mòr with the Outer Hebrides on the horizon

I searched for a way down and soon found the gorge the burger van man had told me about, a deep incision in the hill with a waterfall at its heart. It was a steep descent down a grassy slope where, for the hundredth time, I wished my boots were narrower on my feet to reduce the chance of slipping and a twisted ankle. But thankfully, I made it down without incident, where a bonny mountain stream, Abhainn Scamadal, danced between boulders in a channel fringed with banks of purple heather; in Gaelic, it might be a *gairneag*, a 'noisy little stream'.

Four miles to go.

As if chaperoning me to the finishing line, a flock of geese flew north overhead in an elongated V, honking and chatting as they went. Slipstream stragglers peeled off in groups and surged forward, making a bid for pole position. A letter in the sky continually rewriting itself.

I followed the line of a barbed wire fence due north across a flat bog that sank and rose under my feet like blancmange. After a mile, the fence took flight across an inky-black tributary of the main river. It was half stream, half lake, both flowing through and inhabiting the fen, but I struggled to name it: it didn't feel like a ghyll or a gully, a stream or a brook. In Yorkshire, it might be called a sike, in Gaelic, perhaps a *fèith* or *caochan*. On the map, it was marked 'Abhai n Sneosdal'.

It was too wide to jump, so I leaned over the edge of the marsh grass and lowered my pole to judge the depth. I couldn't feel the bottom, so wading was also discounted. I looked at the wire fence, strung taut about five feet above the water, and considered using it as a climbing frame to bridge the gap, but it was only as high as my waist and topped with barbed wire. It would have been foolish to try, risking damage to myself and the fence. So that just left swimming. The sun was out, but entry and exit would have been tricky, and I wasn't sure I could hurl my backpack across. Running out of direct options, I considered retracing my steps to the base of the cliff and crossing there, but that might have compounded the problem; this tributary joined the main river beyond the fence, which then ran northeast all the way to the coast at Port Gobhlaig. To get around that way, I would have to return almost to the Quiraing and drop down the path to Fingal's tomb. In Scotland, you can walk anywhere but don't know where to walk; in England, you know where to walk but can't walk anywhere.

Having eliminated the impossible, whatever remains is the only credible option. The map showed that the obstructive tributary curved back and around to my left for three miles, where it emanated from Loch Sneosdal, the Snowy Loch. If I followed it far enough, eventually, I'd be able to cross and then retrace my steps on the far side. So, I walked up the spongy river bank, evaluating the width. After about ten minutes, I reached a confluence where two channels joined. There, I hopped across the smaller channel and then hurled my backpack over the second before following it with a standing-start long jump. There was no *splosh*, no cold feet, no impromptu swim. I'd made it.

Drama over, I continued bog hopping over the expanse of mire or *blàr*, aiming for a telecommunications tower on the expansive horizon perched on a hill above Duntulm,

Crossing Abhai n Sneosdal

the only landmark in this featureless flatland, where the landscape was skimmed thin, like butter on toast. It's counterintuitive, but you tend to be able to see further in the lowlands compared with the highlands. Some villages in the Alps lose the sun entirely between November and February due to the towering peaks, and I have a friend who grew up in southern Germany who tells me she couldn't wait to escape the oppression of the surrounding mountains and move north. But most outdoor writers extoll the virtues of lofty scenery over anything else; hundreds of books must have been written on climbing Everest alone. However, a counterpoint to this view is expressed by Noreen Masud, author of *A Flat Place*. I recently attended a talk Noreen gave at the Natural History Museum in Newcastle, where she made an impassioned plea for people to value flatlands that she said are often unloved, marginalised, drained and developed. Directly confronting the obsession of conquering mountains, she said, 'A flat landscape is a means of not having to achieve anything; I can lie down and not have to go anywhere.' She was inspired as a child by seeing glimpses of expansive lush fields outside Lahore as she was driven to school, the only opportunity she had to escape the confines of a house with windows barred for protection. She described actively seeking out flat landscapes in the UK, such as Morecambe Bay, Orford Ness and our very own Town Moor in Newcastle, where she used to live.

Back en route, I, too, slowed down, perhaps because I didn't want my walk to end or the flatness calmed me. I admired the panorama of colourful foliage. Rusty orange spikes of bog asphodel thrust up amongst the cotton grass; sage-green thickets of bog myrtle – the leaves of which are said to ward off midges – stood their ground against the ubiquitous heather that flourished with a million purple bells. Archetypal acidic wetland flora.

*

Eventually, I reached the outer rim of the bog, where I sat on a grassy ledge to eat lunch. Directly ahead, the telecommunications tower, perched on top of a small knoll called Cnoc Roll, kept lookout over the pastoral scene. To the right of the knoll was a collection of white farm buildings around which swirled late-season swallows and house martins that seemed in no rush to migrate south. Sheep dotted the rough green fields, cropping the grass. There was not a single tree to be seen, except for a windbreak of pines around the farm, a feature shared with hill farms along wind-swept Hadrian's Wall. Behind the farm, white sheets flapped on a washing line: Tuesday was washing day.

Lunch over, I scrambled down the ledge where I saw the first signs of human habitation since leaving Portree. The first was a graveyard of 15 rusting bathtubs scattered on the side of a muddy farm track: one still sported shiny chrome taps, but the others stared vacantly at me through holes in their rim like an army of inanimate cybermen.

Beyond the bathtubs, an old red tractor was abandoned on the verge, partly shrouded by bracken. It could have been the prize exhibit of a tractor museum with its tall metal chimney, antique black registration plate, and a pair of beady headlamps. It had no cab, just a horse-like saddle under a thin, elegant steering wheel connected to the front wheels by an external skeletal steering rod: the tractor equivalent of Chitty Chitty Bang Bang.

I walked past the farmhouse where two men were passing sheep through a metal race, possibly for dipping or marking; sheep shuffled in the line, waiting to be processed. Then, a young boy toddled out of the house into the garden and called for his dad, at which the farmer stopped, looked up, and called back like sheep bleating across the fell. Soon, Mother appeared and scooped him up. A fleeting glimpse of family life on Skye, so different to Newcastle, it felt like a page from a storybook. If I'd been invited in to stay for a week, I might have tales to tell to rival Alexander Smith.

I turned the bend and joined a road into Duntulm, the official end of *A Long Walk,* where Paterson promises that the Duntulm Castle Hotel has 'all the usual facilities'. I'd been holding out for a decent coffee, so scouted out the few whitewashed buildings for signs of life: a well-kept bungalow with an oil tank in the back garden; a row of self-catering coastguard cottages overlooking Loch Cleat; a weatherbeaten sign 'Duntulm Castle Hotel' at the top of a drive leading to a dilapidated ruin of a building. *No coffee in Duntulm.*

Pushing the caffeine cravings to the back of my mind, I was lured on by my cliff-top destination at Rubna Hunish and the sight of Duntulm Castle – a ruin on the headland. I edged through a gate and followed a well-worn track to

Tractor near Duntulm

the tumble of stones, but my attention was diverted by a bride and groom running along the clifftop below, holding hands and in full flight, white dress billowing in the breeze. I grabbed my binoculars to confirm this incongruous vignette: a photographer running backwards over the grass a few metres from the cliff edge, a 'best man' shouldering cast-offs. Then, the running stopped, and the bride hitched up her dress, presumably to avoid the mud, revealing black boots and white legs. The foursome marched back up the hill towards the castle, casting long afternoon shadows out to sea.

A few people were already up at the castle, exploring the ruins, where one girl waved out to sea through a window in the rock. She looked north across the Little Minch, as it is known, the stretch of water separating Skye from the Outer Hebrides, where the only clouds in the sky still mirrored the distant mountains. The dashing couple soon arrived for more photos and arranged themselves gaily on the grassy roof of the ruin, with the royal-blue waters of Duntulm Bay in the background.

Down in the bay, the water was crystal and clear. I knelt on the rocks and watched it lap over a liminal garden: ruby-red anemones with outstretched tentacles; emerald-green seaweed good enough to eat; bone-white limpets holding fast; diamond bubbles glistening on the swell. Transformed from liquid jewels to desiccated relics and back twice a day. Life on the edge. Survival. Resilience. Revival.

Wedding photographs at Duntulm Castle

Savouring the moment, I used the lighter gifted to me at The Quiraing and boiled water for a cup of tea. As I drank, the sun sank to about 15 degrees above the horizon, throwing a blinding arc of light across the water. I was grateful for my sunglasses that were back on my head for the first time since Torrin.

After a quick and cooling dip, I had one last task before making the final ascent to journey's end – finding water for my evening meal. I passed one stream that was sluggish and brown, slewing off the fields, but a second, further on, appeared potable, so I used my water filter for the last time to refill my bottles.

As I gained height, a low-lying finger of land came into view: Rubha Hunish. The promontory was bathed in late afternoon sunlight, highlighting the crenelated shoreline that curved backwards and forwards like the hem of the bride's wedding dress. I imagined the inlets being used as beachheads by Viking raiding parties a thousand years ago, sailing down The Minch from their stronghold in the Northern Isles.

I turned around and looked back over the white-washed houses of Duntulm; the grassy knoll topped by the telecommunications tower; the deeply incised gash of Glen Scamadal hiding its secret waterfall; the undulating escarpment rolling south towards the Quiraing. It had been a canny walk.

Ahead was the bothy-on-top-of-the-cliff, shining like a beacon. Inside was a spartan sleeping area and a lookout up front glazed on three sides, once used as a coastguard station. The sun streamed in the window, cooking the inside. A guest book lay open on the window ledge that recounted tales of the many travellers who have taken shelter there. I'd made it: *A Long Walk on the Isle of Skye*!

*

In front of the bothy was a bench with a young man sitting on one side admiring the view and eating his dinner. I asked whether he minded if I joined him, and he turned out to be a fellow hiker I'd briefly met back on the ridge. Not Logan, but an IT consultant from Belgium called Toon. We chattered away about routes and hiking kit while I prepared my meal, and we watched the sun sink behind the Outer Hebrides, turning the sky soft orange, silhouetting the mountains.

I decided to pitch my tent behind the bothy rather than sleep inside, partly to make the most of this dramatic location and also because there were two cyclists staying the night, whose names both began with T: Timu and Tongi, I seem to remember, who had pedalled all the way from Glasgow. They both had long hair and beards and exuded a wild but confident nature. We all sat around sharing leftover items from our packs. There was no wine or beer, but the two Ts brewed a restorative French herbal tea, which was circulated with great reverence, and in turn, they were delighted that I had milk powder left over that they added to their Gallic couscous. These delicacies were followed by chocolate biscuits all round. The time had come to talk of many things: ideas for future expeditions shot back and forth like stars – ski touring in Norway,

Room with a view: Bothy overlooking Rubna Hunish

wandering the Alps, hiking the Hebridean Way. My brain hummed. I felt like I'd found a community I never knew existed except in books and magazines. A diaspora.

At some point, they took to their bunks, and I took to my tent, headtorch on, taking care not to venture over the cliff. Abseiling wasn't on the menu. It was a clear night, and the temperature rapidly dropped to the coldest since my arrival on Skye. I pulled on every layer I had, sacrificing my makeshift pillow: a stuff-sack of spare clothes. I huddled up in my sleeping bag on top of the cliff at Rubna Hunish, wondering if the cabin would have been warmer.

As usual, in the wee small hours of the morning, I woke to answer the call of nature and, using my headtorch for safety, put some distance between myself and the bothy. Then, I switched off my lamp to view the night sky. After a few seconds, my eyes adjusted to the darkness, and I saw Orion with his belt slumped on the horizon and a pin cushion of stars above. There was no moon, so the sky should have been dark, much darker than Newcastle, but there was light pollution on the horizon, bleaching out the picture, and this was odd, because it was the middle of the night. I wondered if there was an airport on Lewis blaring landing lights upwards? The longer I looked, the stranger the light appeared; there were vertical beams and a green haze above the horizon, slightly obscured by the low-lying band of clouds now rendered black. Cold and bleary-eyed, I headed back to the tent, but on a whim, I pulled out my phone to take a picture. The camera automatically activated night mode, so I held it still for a few seconds while it scavenged photons. I looked at the picture: the

Northern Lights! The photograph showed more colours than I could discern with the naked eye, from ghostbusters-green to sickly mauve to dusky red: all the colours of a ripe bruise. Streaks of light shot up from the horizon as if the colours had been run through with a paintbrush. Although I'd seen many photographs of the Northern Lights taken in Northumberland with famous landmarks in the background, such as the recently felled tree at Sycamore Gap, I'd never seen them myself, and being incommunicado for a week, I had no premonition of the phenomenon and was spellbound. As I continued taking photos, trying to hold the camera steady, a ferry with lights blazing sailed westwards along The Minch, contextualising the image.

Before going back to bed, I faced a dilemma. From our conversation that evening, I knew that Toon, Timu, and Tongi would be eager to see the Northern Lights and probably had less chance to do so, living further south. So, I crept into the bothy with my torch obscured and saw them laid out in sleeping bags on the wooded bunks. I made a polite cough, but no one stirred. I coughed again and moved closer. I considered gently shaking them on the shoulder, but in the end, I couldn't bring myself to wake them in the dead of night. After all, I was more or less a perfect stranger, and the lights weren't immediately apparent to the naked eye – especially when half asleep. After playing out the likely conversation the following morning, I let them be and returned to my tent. I opened the vestibule zips on the north side and lay there in silence, allowing my eyes to gradually become more accustomed to the dark and the light. A room with a view.

Northern Lights

10. JOURNEY'S END

I thought Skye had offered up its fair share of wonders, but just before dawn the following morning, all four of us were up early to watch a serene sunrise over the remote hills of Wester Ross to the east. Hoods up, hands in pockets, a chilly spirit of supplication prevailed.

Timu and Tongi were in a contemplative mood that morning, and I discussed plans for returning home with Toon in the comfort of the bothy. Having finished his Skye Trail a day earlier than expected, he planned to catch the bus south to visit the site of the dinosaur footprints on Trotternish's east coast. We checked the times on the website and determined to walk back to Duntulm together as I was taking the same bus to Portree, from where I thought I could catch another bus to Armadale and retrace my steps home. Timu and Tongi came in at some point, and we reminisced about our journeys. At first, I didn't mention my experience in the night for fear of bragging, but as the conversation wound on, one of them asked me if I was cold in the tent, and he thought he had heard me investigating the bothy. So, I spilled the beans.

Sunrise on the final day

They were magnanimous throughout and enjoyed looking at my photos. Then Timu told us about a hilarious expedition the pair did to Norway in the summer a few years ago. Tongi had asked him to research how to get good photos of the Northern Lights, so he worked out the correct settings and packed his best camera, but after the first day of trekking through the wilderness, they realised seeing them would be impossible due to the 24-hours of sunlight! So, by way of consolation, I suggested that they set their alarms for 2am that night and point their cameras north if they were still in the area, just in case. I hope they saw them.

I had always imagined that before I departed Rubna Hunish, I would climb down the steep path carved into the cliff, like Toon had done before I arrived and walk the mile to the northern tip of the peninsula and commune with the elements. But in the end, I was enjoying the company of my fellow travellers so much that I didn't get around to it. The time just slid away. Delightfully. All too soon, we said our goodbyes, and Toon and I trotted back to Duntulm and flagged down the bus heading south.

Journey's end.

*

Skye had been a great adventure – seven days hiking across some of the wildest and most rugged terrain of my life. Although I'd spent much time on my own away from the chatter of everyday life – and experienced that whole-body enema Stephen King describes in *The Stand* – what struck me the most as the bus trundled down the road to Portree was the kindness of strangers: the young couple on the beach at Ord who sent a message to Tracy to tell her I was safe; the man with the camper van at Torrin who raided his small fridge so I didn't go hungry; the hostel that found me a bed for the night; the receptionist at the Cuillin Hills Hotel who willingly took receipt of my resupply parcel; and of course, my German friend at the Quiraing who gave me his only lighter so I could cook. It all reminded me of how people had rallied in support when my good friend Dorothy was dying in 2019. Vulnerability is a prerequisite for grace.

Looking north to Rubna Hunish and the Outer Hebrides

APPENDIX 1: KIT LIST

On the run-up to my trip to Skye, I tried to lighten my load. My previous base weight was around 10kg, and I got this down to 7.1kg, which felt like a considerable reduction on my back. In addition, my worn weight, including trekking poles, was 1.9kg, and at the beginning, I also carried around 1.6kg of food and up to 2kg of water. I saved carrying half my food by posting a resupply parcel ahead to Portree. Sometimes, I only carried 1kg of water if I knew there were plenty of streams ahead.

All outdoor kit decisions are a balance between durability, weight and cost, and here, I summarise my thoughts about how each item I carried performed on Skye.

Boots:
It seems increasingly common for through-hikers and fastpackers to wear trail shoes rather than boots (yes, I can image Wainwright turning in his grave), and although I wear trail shoes for fell running, I feel anxious when not wearing boots on a long hike due to the risk of uneven ground, spiky vegetation, and the prospect

of walking for days on end with damp feet. One hiker I met on Skye countered this problem with waterproof socks, but I imagine they can get very sweaty. When fell-running, I concentrate on my foot placement, planning two or three steps ahead, but when hiking I want to look at the view, so I need more sturdy footwear.

With this in mind, I purchased a pair of lightweight boots from **Inov-8**, the **Roclite G400 GTX** (v1). They are super light for a boot, only weighing 426g each. This compares to 785g for my regular leather Zamberlan boots and 433g for my Trespass walking shoes. The outdoor writer Chris Townsend said that weight on your foot feels like double the weight elsewhere, so lighter footwear makes a big difference on a long hike. I paid £60 for these at the Inov-8 factory shop in Crook. As well as being light, they have a tough graphene sole with deep studs and a waterproof Gore-Tex liner. I'm always suspicious of waterproof claims for non-leather boots, but I was surprised how well these remained waterproof over 85 miles of wet grass and bog on Skye. They were also relatively cool in the heat. However, my big problem with these boots, as I described in my narrative, is their immense width, coupled with the poor tongue and lace mechanism that starts halfway up the foot, making them impossible to tighten effectively if you have a narrow foot. I tried adding various insoles, but they only pushed my foot up to the top of the boot, doing nothing to make the boot narrower.

If you have a wide foot, these boots might be ideal, but they risked injury on every steep camber for me. Inov-

8 uses a width scale from 1 to 5 but produces each model only in a single width. The Roclite G400 V1 GTX are sold as width 4; however, I noticed that version 2 of these boots are billed as having a wraparound heel lock system for increased stability, so this might be an improvement. By contrast, I also have the Inov-8 Roclite G275 trail running shoes, which, at width 3, fit perfectly, giving me increased confidence when running off-road.

Although my boots remained waterproof and the grip underfoot was superb, cosmetically, they didn't wear particularly well with tears around the rim of the sole (there *are* lots of sharp rocks on Skye) and parts of the upper pulled away from the sole, probably due to the poor fit and lateral stress. If Inov-8 ever produce a similar boot with a width of 3, I'd try them.

Hiking Poles:

My hiking poles are trusty **Black Diamonds** weighing 450g for the pair. I've had these for years, and I can't fault them. Occasionally, I've fallen on one hard, and it's flexed but never snapped – they seem indestructible. Also, unlike some poles, the locking system is a latch rather than a barrel, making it easy and quick to use. My poles are the same as those used by Keith Foskett when he hiked the Pacific Crest Trail, and he nicknamed his 'Click and Clack' because of the sound they made striking the ground. Tragically, Foskett describes in his book, *The Last Englishman*, how Clack got stuck in a rock when crossing a fast-flowing river, Dingley Creek, and was washed away. He wrote: 'Click and I watched despondently as our companion bobbed into the distance. Our hearts sank. We turned north, paused for one last glimpse and left.' If the same happened to me on Skye, it would have spelt 'disaster' because my hiking poles were essential for my tent.

Backpack:

Montane, Trailblazer 44L. This pack weighs 995g, an incredible 705g lighter than my previous pack, the rugged North Face Terra 55L. I was fortunate to find an ex-photoshoot Trailblazer for £60 in the Montane factory shop in Ashington; the full price is around £125 at the time of writing. I was tempted to purchase this pack after outdoor writer Alex Roddie praised the 30L version for its close-fitting design following fastpacking the Grande Traversata Delle Alpi in 2022. As soon as I tried it on in the shop, I knew it was for me, feeling more like an item of clothing than a rucksack. By contrast, I loathe banana-shaped rucksacks with over-engineered curved frames that transfer all the weight to your lower vertebrae and pack like a snail shell; I'd rather have a sweaty back. With two sternum straps, the Trailblazer pulls tight, dissipates the load and doesn't jiggle about. It also has a semi-rigid back panel covered in mesh to provide stability that ultra-light packs don't have. It's a perfect balance between features and weight.

I only had two problems with this pack. Firstly, on my second or third practice outing, the thin tether that secures the right shoulder strap to the top of the pack completely gave way from where it was stitched into the back panel. This would have been a disaster had it happened on Skye because I doubt I'd have been able to repair it with my miniature sewing kit. But credit to the staff at Montane in Ashington, they took it back and repaired it within a week, re-sewing both the tethers and making them twice as strong. I'm happy to say I had no other manufacturing problems despite giving the pack some pounding over the week.

My second complaint (that I've since resolved) are the side pockets. Rather than being stretchy like every other rucksack I've seen, they have no give, and therefore, it's almost impossible to squeeze in a water bottle if the pack is stuffed without taking the skin off your fingers. I saw this as a potential problem even before I bought it, and the shop assistant recommended inserting water bottles before packing; however, this is impractical on the side of a mountain when refilling your water bottles in a gale. An unusual feature of this pack is that it has two additional wrap-around side pockets facing forward to allow access to essentials such as suncream and midge repellent whilst walking – providing you have highly articulate wrists. Ironically, it was only after I got home and was unpacking that I realised these horizontal access pockets were large enough to fit 1L water bottles. You just need to make sure that the tops are screwed on securely so they don't leak.

Rather than covering my pack with a waterproof cover, I used an Exped internal liner for my sleeping bag and spare clothes. I'd read that stuffing all your items in a single bag saves a lot of space compared with using lots of separate stuff sacs – and it does!

I also used two or three small Osprey dry bags for smaller items I wanted to keep separate. This worked well, except for when it rained heavily, and my matches got ruined in a non-waterproof ditty bag. Lesson learnt.

Tent:

Tarptent, Notch Li. Wow, what a tent! It's not cheap (costing me $649, plus $49 shipping, plus £120 in tax on delivery, totalling £672), but it is light, weighing in at a featherweight 607g, including stakes and bag. I swapped out the four supplied pegs with ten sturdy V-shaped stakes, increasing the total weight to 645g, but it was still 555g lighter than my previous Vango (F10). I've had the F10 out in all weathers in Cumbria and found it to be virtually bomb-proof, so it was a risk swapping a traditional nylon tunnel tent for ephemeral Dyneema (DCF), but I didn't regret my decision. In fact, I revelled not only in the lightness of the Notch Li but also its speed of pitching, waterproofness, lack of fabric sag, and double vestibules that are great for storing gear, as well as dawn and dusk views.

I thoroughly researched Dyneema trekking pole tents and boiled it down to the Notch Li or the Durston X-Mid Pro 1. The latter has a cleaver asymmetric design, increasing internal space, but I went for the Notch because I wanted the security of a full mesh inner, whereas the Durston is partially single skin. My decision was heavily influenced by long-distance hiker Mark Webb and his review of using the Notch Li extensively in the UK. He concluded that it was his perfect lightweight tent, but added an update after 100 nights that it showed signs of wear and needed patching on the Cape Wrath Trail. Dyneema is very strong but tends to delaminate over time. This didn't seem like a problem for me because, due to work commitments, I'd be a very happy camper if I get to spend 100 nights in a tent over the next few years.

A drawback of the Notch Li is its pack size. Dyneema is light but doesn't pack small. You roll it up around two 41 cm rigid struts into a bulky sausage that slips into the tent bag. I had a moment of panic that it wouldn't fit into my new backpack until I devised a way of squeezing it into the roll-up hood by stretching the backpack fabric. For some people, it might also be a problem that the fabric is slightly transparent, but I was happy to be woken up at dawn, and an eye mask would easily solve this problem in mid-summer. Also, as I was sleeping in the wild, privacy wasn't a problem, and the semi-solid mesh inner also helped in this respect.

I agonised about the need for a groundsheet. Under FAQs, Tarptent says the 1-oz Dyneema flooring is tough and doesn't usually require a separate groundsheet as long as the ground is clear of sharp objects. Ultimately, I didn't take a groundsheet and had no problems as I was mostly camping on grass. I was amazed at how waterproof the groundsheet was during my night at Bealach na Bèiste, where I camped in a bog and could see the water moving under the tent. It was cold but not wet. In contrast, the floor on Durston's X-Mid Pro 1 is made of silnylon (probably for increased puncture resistance), but they are introducing a lighter Dyneema floor option in 2024.

I made one modification to the Notch Li by adding four additional tie-off points to the base of the flysheet to reduce flapping and increase stability (the tent is only supplied with four tie-off points around the base, plus two guy lines from the ridge). I purchased DCF self-adhesive tie-out patches from **Wild Sky Gear** for a few pounds each. Unlike silicon-coated fabrics, DCF is very receptive to patching in this way. When pitching, I was careful not to over-tighten these tie-outs so as not to distort the intended structure of the tent, but they did help to reduce flapping around the base of the fly sheet, and I was very grateful for them during my night in the storm.

If I could make one design improvement to the Notch Li, it would be to increase the depth of the slots into which your upturned trekking poles fit. This is the structural weak point in high winds, and an extra few millimetres would make all the difference. I countered this problem by ensuring the poles were fully tensioned.

I carried a small flannel to wipe any moisture off the inside and outside of my tent (20g). However, I didn't get much condensation on the inside, and rain runs off the outside of Dyneema like water off a duck's back.

Sleeping bag:
When I started backpacking around Northumberland in 2019, I shivered every night in an army surplus bivvy bag paired with a Mountain Warehouse sleeping bag weighing 870g, which was little better than a bin liner. After three summers, I realised the bag contained almost

no stuffing, so upgraded to the **Robens Couloir 350**. By contrast, Couloir is like sleeping in a luxury hotel with super soft down. It squashes down small and fluffs up big; it is sold as weighing 795g, but mine weighs 829g without the stuff sack. It is a 3-season bag with an advertised temperature limit of -4C for men and 2C for women. It is much warmer than my old bag, but if I expected the temperature to fall below freezing, I would add a thermal liner.

Two other things I love about this sleeping bag are the central zip and the colour. I struggled with a bag zip on the opposite side of my bivvy zip for two years, so a central zip solves that problem. It also makes sense when sleeping in it, especially when it is hot. The bag is a lively gold colour, which I wouldn't have selected had there been a choice, but I find it cheered up inside my tent, especially when cold and windy.

Sleeping mat:
I have used the **Sea to Summit, Ultralight Insulated Air** for the last four years, and it's stood the test of time. The waffle design makes it comfortable and keeps me warm enough from underneath. It weighs 430g and includes a bag with a pump-sack. It is pretty thin at 5cm but has a good R-value of 3.1 (the higher, the better). If expecting sub-zero temperatures, I would take a reflective foil layer mat to put underneath the airbed for extra insulation. I've had no punctures, but carry the repair kit in case.

Sleeping clothes:

I carry a layer of clothes to sleep in that I pack inside my sleeping bag and dry sack. On this trip, I took a **Tog 24 Polartec top** (185g) and **Montane Dart Thermo Baselayer trousers** (176g). These items were overkill for the heatwave on the first few days, but proved essential by the end of the week.

Cooking:

Back in 2019, I scavenged my old Trangia from the loft when hiking up the Northumberland coast. It's a robust stove, built to last, and is windproof, but weighs a hefty 770g, plus a meths bottle. In 2020, I switched to gas, purchased a tiny **MSR burner** with integrated ignition that weighs only 83g, and paired it with a **Toaks 750ml titanium pot** at 123g. To reduce the risk of causing wildfires, I use foldout feet for the gas canister (32g), so a total weight of 238g, excluding gas.

All went well with this system until the night I cooked in a storm at Bealach na Bèiste on Skye. I'd packed an aluminium foil sheet to use as a windguard that I wrapped around the burner, securing it with copper wire. It did its job, preventing the wind from blowing out the flame and all was going well until I heard a pop. The reflected heat had blown the ignition. After that incident, I relied on a few spare matches, which got soaked and wouldn't light.

Eating and drinking:

I usually eat my breakfast in a small plastic bowl (60g). I could also eat from my titanium cooking pot, but it's an awkward shape and difficult to clean. But, to save weight on this trip, I purchased a pack of five **silver foil cake containers** from a local hardware shop for £5 and took just one, weighing 10g. Tracy thought it would leak, and it did after getting squashed in my pack, but not until the penultimate day.

I used a slide-out plastic spoon from Optimus that weighs 24g, to eat. It slides out to 23cm, so it is handy for reaching the bottom of freeze-dried meal packs. It worked well and didn't break; I preferred it to a traditional spork, which I dislike the feel of in my mouth.

Due to the narrow side pockets in my Montane backpack, I purchased two soft plastic water bottles that I planned to squish into the limited space, but I rejected them after a few trials: I found them difficult to fill and clean out and worried about the growth of bacteria. So, I purchased two 1L sugary fruit drinks at the last minute, poured out the contents, and filled them with water. They weighed just 26g each, which compares to 126g each for my regular water bottles.

My water filter for Skye was **Alpkit's Hippo Compact** (121g including fill-bladder). This lovely little gravity filter was much easier to use than my previous pump-action MSR Trailshot Microfilter, which was agonizing on my wrists after filling a few bottles. With the Hippo, I just fill the bladder from the stream with dirty water, attach it to the filter, and dangle over my water bottle using the straw provided to direct the flow.

Once a day, I added an **electrolyte tablet** to my water bottle (Phizz 3-in-1 formula). Typically, when walking in hot weather, I suffer from headaches no matter how much I drink, but I didn't have this problem on Skye. It might have been a coincidence, but I put it down to these tablets, each of which contained 319mg of Sodium, 115mg of Potassium, and 229mg of Chloride and had a pleasant apple and blackcurrant taste.

Waterproofs:

I'd never owned a dedicated lightweight hiking waterproof top, so on discovering the Montane factory shop near Newcastle, I bought their **Pac Plus jacket** that weighs just 285g (by way of comparison, my old waterproof jacket was from Trespass and weighs 528g). It is short and light, but I found it an impermeable, windproof shell. It is more robust than a featherweight cycling or fellrunning top, but thinner than a winter cagoule. It was perfect in every way and rolled up tight. I paid £110 for this item.

The oldest item I took on this trip was my **Berghaus waterproof trousers** (Gore-Tex Paclite) that weigh 216g. I paid about £100 for these ten years ago. Although they have been re-waterproofed many times, they have stood the test of time and only recently begun to show signs of wear, and one of the zips has failed.

Walking clothes:

I am inseparable from my favourite **long-sleeved hiking** top that I've had for years, by Tog 24. It is made from a comfortable waffle fabric, has stretch panels under the arms, and a very long neck zip. I've not been able to find anything remotely as good since buying it, and Tog has discontinued the design, but even after hundreds of washes, it is still as good as new. It weighs 256g, and the label reads 'Polartec Classic'.

My backup top for Skye was from Montane, the gossamer thin **short-sleeve Dart Nano Zip** that weighs almost nothing (75g) on my scales. This top was a lifesaver during the hot weather, and I'd regularly take it off, dip it in a stream, wring it out, and put it back on wet. It is zingy electric blue, so stands out on the mountain and gives me a lift.

At the risk of sounding like Montane-man, my trousers were their **Terra Pants** at 350g. They were the perfect thickness for this trip (thin, but not like tracing paper) and have a minimalist integrated belt that didn't conflict with the hip belt on my rucksack. When it was hot, I opened the thigh vents. I could have also rolled them up, but didn't want to increase my risk of ticks, so they stayed tucked into my socks that were treated with Permethrin.

My jacket was another old favourite item of clothing: a hooded **Regatta softshell** in black and red with a large internal map pocket. It is stretchy and easy to walk or run in, contains some insulation, and is relatively windproof. It is pretty heavy at 401g, but as I didn't take a down jacket on this trip, it got a lot of wear in the mornings and evenings. Before this trip, I enjoyed repairing the seams with customised red stitching; it wouldn't qualify me for *The Great British Sewing Bee,* but did the job.

In addition, I took two pairs of socks (Bridgedale 53g and Regatta 68g), three pairs of Wirarpa modal briefs (62g each), a hat (62g), a snood (54g), two hankies (16g each), a thin pair of gloves (26g), and, of course, the essential mosquito hood (24g).

Luxuries:

When I'm packing for a trip, a scene from Cheryl Strayed's book *Wild* plays in my mind. After lugging her pack 'Monster' for several weeks to the first staging post at Kennedy Meadows, a fellow hiker, Albert, helps to reduce the weight by systematically questioning every item: foldable saw, miniature binoculars, megawatt flash for camera, disposable razors, condoms? The only item I carried across Skye on that list was my small pair of **Delta binoculars**, weighing 238g, without which I'd feel half-naked.

My other luxury was my **Kindle** (157g) on which I was reading *The Stand* by Stephen King, an epic tale about a deadly virus that wipes out 99% of the population of America and evolves into a modern-day biblical saga of good versus evil. Coincidentally, there is plenty of hiking in the book as a small band of unlikely heroes trek across the Rocky Mountains to confront the villains in Las Vegas.

Some might also consider my sit mat, weighing 23g, a luxury.

Swimming:

You might put these items in the category of luxuries, but for swimming (an activity that also doubles up as washing), I carried a pair of **Nike** brief-lined racing shorts that weigh 103g. These could have also doubled up as an emergency pair of shorts, if absolutely necessary, but I wouldn't have wanted to model them in Glasgow on a Saturday night.

A decent towel is essential for drying off after a cold water swim, and the lightest towel for its size is the **Lightload Beach Towel,** made from natural materials that I discovered on **Wild Sky Gear's** website. It is a massive 1.5m x 90cm but only weighs 134g. I agree, it's unusual to carry a beach-sized towel on a thru-hike, and I considered cutting it in half to save weight, but it felt so good to have a wraparound towel after a swim I kept it whole. When the towel arrived in the post, I thought Wild Sky Gear had made a mistake because it came in a pack the size of a small wallet. To expand it, I had to soak it in water, where, like the Lambton Worm, it 'grew and grew to an aaful size'.

On previous trips, I've also taken a pair of sea goggles that weigh 140g, but this time, I left them at home. But, when I swam off a beautiful white-sand beach on my first day in the sunshine, I wished I'd packed them to look at the fish.

Electronics:
On previous trips, I've taken a small Canon camera (PowerShot SX230 HS) with a 14x optical zoom, weighing 220g. This had three advantages over using a mobile phone for photography: the tiny battery lasted forever, and I also carried a few spares, so no battery anxiety; the 14x zoom meant I could take photos of wildlife close-up, albeit of poor quality; it can be easily operated with one

hand whilst walking. However, in 2023, I purchased a **Samsung S22 Galaxy** phone (245g) that takes superior pictures to my old point-and-shoot. So, reluctantly, I purchased a **10k Belkin power pack** (208g) and hoped I'd have enough juice to use my phone as a camera for the week. I missed the 14x zoom, but the S22 does have a dedicated 3x lens that helps for distance shots. I suffered battery anxiety at first, but found that if I kept the phone on flight mode, the battery didn't drain too quickly, if I only used the camera. I set the phone battery to the 'saver' setting so that it didn't charge beyond 85% (the last 15% is an inefficient use of power) and found that on a typical day, taking around 100 photos, the charge would drop to approximately 30%. In this way, I could charge up my phone four times with the power pack. Because I also stopped for a night in the hostel at Portree, where I charged everything, in the end, I had plenty of power for the week. I referred to my phone occasionally for navigation but mainly used a map and compass. I also sent the occasional text message. The fastest battery drain on my phone occurred when I left the mobile data on in an often vain attempt to get a signal. For this reason, I am considering purchasing a Garmin inReach Mini satellite communicator for future trips. *Tracy **adds**: please do and then I can see where you are even if you can't get a phone signal.*

I had intended to purchase a modern **headtorch** before this September trip, but in the end, I didn't get around to it, so stuck with my cheap plastic hardware version that cost £5, weighing 107g. It is temperamental, and occasionally bits fall off, but I carried **Gaffer Tape** for running repairs. It is necessary to remove the battery before packing; otherwise, it can switch itself on.

As mentioned above, I also took my **Kindle** (157g), which has a backlight, so I can read it without using the battery on the headtorch.

First aid and personal items:

I took a small first aid kit that weighed around 150g in a Dyneema ditty bag. This included a small foldup toothbrush that Tracy found for me, a 5ml tube of travel toothpaste, 18ml midge-repellent by Smidge, a tick-removal tool, plasters, tissues, blister plasters, Blistex lip cream, painkillers, and various potions and lotions, such as Ibuprofen gel and Savlon. I decanted the lotions into tiny 3 or 5ml plastic cosmetics containers that I found on Amazon, saving a lot of weight compared with full tubes. If you do this, I recommend labelling each tub; otherwise, you might mistake something like Ibuprofen gel for pile cream.

In addition, I took suncream (60g), hand gel (38g), a Swiss Army Knife (100g), and prescription Sunglasses (75g).

Navigation:

In preparation for this trip, I purchased the **OS 1:50,000 maps** for North and South Skye and highlighted the route as accurately as possible from David Paterson's description in *A Long Walk*. With much chagrin, I cut out the highlighted sections into small sheets and numbered them in order. All the sheets weighed 70g, while the two complete maps weighed 192g, so cutting the maps up saved 122g.

I also plotted the route on the **OS map app** and downloaded it to my phone. Therefore, I could have risked not taking the paper maps and saved 70g, but 40+ years of mountain experience told me that would be foolish, and it would also have drained my phone's battery more by constantly referring to the online map. In any case, I enjoy navigating with a map and compass. However, sometimes, I would view the map on my phone to see greater detail at a 1:25,000 scale; I also occasionally checked my position, especially when walking in the clouds.

I used a small **Silva compass** weighing 25g.

My hiking kit

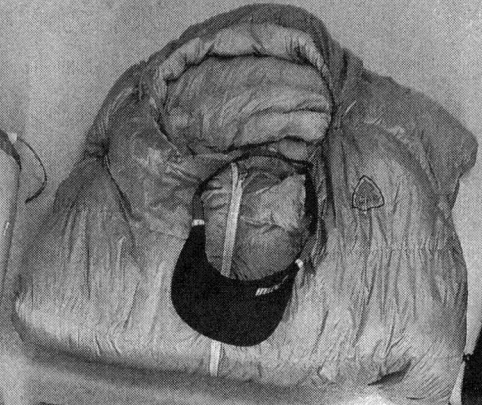

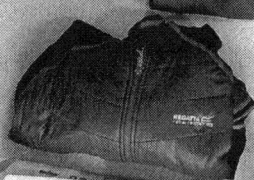

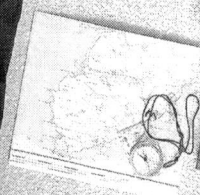

APPENDIX 2: ROUTE DETAILS

The route I took was first proposed by David Paterson in his photobook, *A Long Walk on the Isle of Skye*, published in 1999 by Peak Publishing. The walk starts at Armadale on the south coast (facilitating use of the Mallaig ferry) and officially finishes on the north coast at Duntulm, although Paterson recommends exploring the dramatic headland of Rubha Hunish, which adds an extra couple of miles. Paterson states that the total distance to Duntulm was 75 miles, but using the OS map app, I calculated that I walked 82 miles to Duntulm, with 13,418 ft of ascent.

You can view and download my route from the OS Map App. Either use the following hyperlink or search on the app for my 84-mile route starting in Armadale. Link: https://explore.osmaps.com/route/18639634/a-long-walk-on-skye-sept-2023?lat=57.402391&lon=-6.389752&zoom=8.9624&style=Leisure&type=2d

In *A Long Walk*, Paterson provides a route description and distance for each day. In the table below, I have listed

Paterson's start and end points for each day, his distance
(DP), my calculated distance (MB), and my calculated
ascent. The first table is in miles and feet, and the second
table is in kilometres and metres.

	Start	Finish	Distance DP (miles)	Distance MB (miles)	Distance MB (total miles)	Ascent (ft)
Day 1	Armadale Pier	Ord	11.8	12.7	12.7	1,531
Day 2	Ord	Heaste	9.3	8.8	21.5	608
Day 3	Heaste	Torrin	9	9	30.5	1,099
Day 4	Torrin	Sligachan	9.3	10.5	41	2,032
Day 5	Sligachan	Portree	11.2	12	53	912
Day 6	Portree	The Storr CP	7.8	9	62	1,733
Day 7	The Storr CP	Quiraing CP	12.7	14	76	3,988
Day 8	Quiraing CP	Duntulm	5.6	6	82	1,117
	Duntulm	Rubha Hunish		2	84	398

	Start	Finish	Distance DP (km)	Distance MB (km)	Distance MB (total km)	Ascent (m)
Day 1	Armadale Pier	Ord	19	20.4	20.4	467
Day 2	Ord	Heaste	15	14.1	34.6	180
Day 3	Heaste	Torrin	14.5	14.5	49	335
Day 4	Torrin	Sligachan	15	16.9	66	619
Day 5	Sligachan	Portree	18	19.3	85.3	278
Day 6	Portree	The Storr CP	12.5	14.5	99.8	528
Day 7	The Storr CP	Quiraing CP	20.5	22.5	122.3	1,318
Day 8	Quiraing CP	Duntulm	9	9.7	132	340
	Duntulm	Rubha Hunish		3.2	135.2	121

Paterson aimed to finish each day at a village or somewhere accessible by road, whereas I aimed to camp somewhere relatively remote. As a result, I completed the walk in seven, rather than eight days, by walking from Heaste to Portree in two days and camping at the mountain pass Bealach na Bèiste. Both Paterson and I took half a day off in Portree to recuperate.

As I explain in my narrative, parts of the route are hard going and involve miles of pathless terrain. On Sleat, the difficulty is compounded by dense vegetation, deep gorges and deer fences. After a lovely start crossing the

189

Sleat peninsula and descending into the wooded vale of Meadhonach, you reach the west coast at six miles, where there are sandy beaches. There is a pathless couple of miles to Achnacloich (8.5 miles), where you join the road to Ord (13 miles).

The most difficult section of the walk is from Ord to Boreraig, along the south shore of Loch Eilean, where it took me ten hours to walk 11 miles. On departing Ord, you are faced with a choice: navigate the rocky beach or contour around the side of the mountain. The beach is very uneven, and there are several cliffs, so I got pushed uphill by the terrain. I then had to cross several deep gorges, two of which are marked on the map as Garbh Allt at 14.5 miles and Allt a' Chinn Mhoir at 15.5 miles. If I did the walk again, I would probably try to hug the shoreline at low tide, although I did enjoy exploring the unnamed lichen-clad woods.

Paterson warns not to attempt crossing the head of Loch Eilean at the muddy delta but to continue up the river, called Abhainn Ceann, for a short distance where a crossing can be made at just under 19 miles. Depending on the depth of water, your feet may get wet.

The north shore of Loch Eilean is a little easier because there are no cliffs, although there are a few scrambles, and you will probably be exhausted by the time you reach Heaste (21.5 miles). From Heaste, Paterson advises taking an old track out of the village that heads over the hill called Meall Buaile nan Caorach, rather than following the coast. I located the track just across the ford to the east of the village, but it soon petered out a mile up the hill. A high deer fence bisects the mountain, which must be climbed before descending steeply in deep vegetation to Boreraig at 24 miles. Boreraig is a beautiful grassy spot with running water and space to camp, a reward after strenuous endeavours, and there is also a beautiful waterfall on the shore to the east.

After Boreraig, the going becomes much easier as the route merges with the official Skye Trail until Torrin (31 miles). After Torrin, the route diverges from The Skye Trail, crossing the mountains via a pass called Bealach na Bèiste, before dropping down into Glen Sligachan. There is a tricky section of navigation between Bealach na Bèiste (34 miles) and Druim Eadar Da Choire (35 miles) or Point 489, as it is marked on the OS map. At first, you follow a broken fence on the south flank of Garbh-bheinn marked on the 1:25,000 scale OS map. Where the fence kinks left, uphill, you carry on contouring around the mountain, passing beneath Point 489 until access can be gained to the ridge up a steep grass slope before doubling back to Point 489. From Point 489, you follow another ruined fence due west towards a col between Garbh-bheinn and Marsco, marked Point 323 on the OS map. From there, it is all downhill, contouring around the heathery flank of Marsco until the well-trodden path in Glen Sligachan is gained at 38 miles.

The next 39 miles to the Quiraing follows the same route as The Skye Trail, and although there aren't dedicated trail signposts, you're mainly walking on minor roads or well-worn tracks, so there are no navigational difficulties so long as you don't stray too close to the edge of the escarpment in bad weather. From the Sligachan Hotel (41 miles), follow the north shore of Loch Sligachan to the village of Peinchorran (44 miles) and then the road to Portree (53 miles). I discovered that it is common for folks walking The Skye Trail to get a bus down the A87 from Portree to the Sligachan Hotel to miss this section entirely. However, I wouldn't recommend doing that on *The Long Walk* because it would spoil the fun of walking continuously from the south to the north coast of Skye. Also, I found the minor road a welcome change of pace.

From Portree, follow the coastal escarpment to The Storr car park (62 miles), then relish the main section of the breathtaking Trotternish Ridge to the Quiraing car park (76 miles), praying you get good weather.

From the Quiraing car park, you can take the lower or higher path. The lower path meanders around the famous rock formations, while the higher path looks down on them. Paterson took the higher path, and so did I, reaching the trig point on the summit of Meall na Suiramach. If you take the lower path, after passing The Needle and The Table, you will reach Fir Bhreugach, where a path doubles back up the mountain, joining *The Long Walk* route. If I did the walk again, I'd take the lower path to get a better view of the rock formations.

There are no paths for the next four miles to the outskirts of Duntulm, but there is an amazing view. From the summit of Meall na Suiramach, contour along the western side of the boggy ridge until you reach the summit of Sgùrr Mòr, where, on a clear day, you will see the whole northern tip of the peninsula. From there, drop steeply down the east side of Glen Scamadal (79 miles), which hides an impressive waterfall. Next, I followed the west bank of the River Scamadal towards Duntulm but had to make a tricky river crossing. Alternatively, you could stay on the east side of the river and locate the footbridge Paterson mentioned in *A Long Walk* near to the village of Conasta. I only noticed that Paterson used a footbridge to cross the river after I returned home and reread his book; I then located the bridge on the 1:25,000 scale OS map at grid reference NG 43304 72806. Whichever route you take from Glen Scamadal to Duntulm, you must negotiate a large, flat, boggy fen. Pack a spare pair of socks, just in case.

From Duntulm (82 miles), head to the coast and explore the ruins of Duntulm Castle before skirting around Duntulm Bay and ascending the final hill to the wonderfully remote clifftop bothy overlooking Rubha Hunish. A fine place to finish a long walk!

I'd love to hear about your experience if you try this route. You can find me on X (formerly known as Twitter) @marekbidwell.

ACKNOWLEDGEMENTS

E ven though this is a relatively short book, it has been a long time in the making. That journey began when I started school and struggled to read and write. The very thought of 'spelling tests' still fills me with horror to this day. These days, I might have been diagnosed with dyslexia. I remember my mother, who was a primary school teacher, patiently reading *James and the Giant Peach* with me every evening one holiday: a long slog for both of us. But she didn't give up. In fact, she went on to specialise in teaching children with dyslexia and used many of those skills to help me. Likewise, my father, who taught computing, wrote a programme on our ZX Spectrum in the early 1980s to help me prepare for those dreaded spelling tests. Each word flashed briefly on the screen, and I had to type it in. If I got the correct answer, a pleasant sound played along with a word of praise; incorrect, and the machine buzzed and spat out a random amusing insult, like 'A monkey could do better'! At the age of seven or eight, I found this hilarious, and there was probably no better way to help me memorise those spellings. So, thank you to Susan and Lionel Bidwell.

Despite dyslexic tendencies, I've always loved stories and books – gateways into other worlds – and especially discussing them with others. These discussions have, in turn, sparked my own writing. I've been a member of *The Shakespeare Book Club* in Heaton since its inception in 2009, so thank you to members, past and present, for your inspiration, debate, and exposing me to new ways of thinking. So far, we've read more than 90 books together. My favourites include *Number 9 Dream* by David Mitchell, *All The Light You Cannot See* by Anthony Doerr and *The Salt Path* by Raynor Winn.

Before writing this book, I wrote another about a long walk around Northumberland. Several friends and colleagues kindly read that first attempt and gave me invaluable comments. Although that book remains unpublished, your feedback has shaped my writing and, therefore, this book. So, a great big thank you to Rob Wallace, Andrew Keyes, Richard Clarke, Sharon Maguire, Robert McKibbin, Tom Carlisle and Alex Roddie for your support and encouragement in my writing journey. A description of my Northumberland walk was published in the February/March 2022 edition of *The Northumbrian* magazine. Hopefully, I will return to *A Northumbrian Odyssey* one day.

My wife, Tracy Bidwell, has patiently read, corrected spelling mistakes, and helped me in many ways with all my writing, as well as supporting my hiking adventures. She also painted the stunning cover for this book – see @TracyBidwell in Instagram for more of her work. Thank you, Tracy, I'm overjoyed to have shared my life with you Xxx.

Thank you to all the people I met on the Isle of Skye who helped me along the way, whether filling my water bottles, offering food or a cigarette lighter, giving directions, or sending messages to Tracy on my behalf.

Although I never met him, I wouldn't have completed this walk without the inspiration of photographer David Paterson, author of *A Long Walk on the Isle of Skye*. While writing this book, I sought to contact him but discovered he sadly passed away in 2023. Still, I found a glowing obituary of him on the website of 'Little Sparta', a Scottish garden in the Pentland Hills that he photographed, describing his life and works.

Three other outdoor writers or photographers also particularly inspired me with this project: Quintin Lake – who walked the coast of Britain between 2015 and 2020 and published hundreds of sublime photographs on his website *THE PERIMETER* – encouraged me to 'keep writing' over a coffee in Newcastle; Alex Roddie, author of *The Farthest Shore*, who has long been an inspiration, gave me advice both on writing and lightweighting my kit; and Robert Macfarlane – whose treasure trove of a book *Landmarks* was my ever-present writing companion, and my copy of which is now dog-eared and highlighted – taught me to think more deeply about landscapes, and the words that describe them, *'Language carries a formative as well as an informative impulse'*.

Finally, thank you to Lead Editor Ruth Lunn and Designer Jay Thompson at UK Book Publishing for editing and bringing this book to life.